No Such Thing
as Can't

No Such Thing as Can't

One Man's Journey Across the Southern Seas and through Poverty and Ordeals to Become One of Indonesia's Most Prominent Bankers

Dahlan Iskan

iUniverse, Inc.
Bloomington

No Such Thing as Can't
One Man's Journey Across the Southern Seas and through Poverty and Ordeals to
Become One of Indonesia's Most Prominent Bankers

iUniverse books may be ordered through booksellers or by contacting:

iUniverse
1663 Liberty Drive
Bloomington, IN 47403
www.iuniverse.com
1-800-Authors (1-800-288-4677)

ISBN: 978-1-4620-1923-6 (sc)
ISBN: 978-1-4620-1924-3 (hc)
ISBN: 978-1-4620-1925-0 (ebk)

Library of Congress Control Number: 2011906884

Printed in the United States of America

iUniverse rev. date: 10/31/2011

CONTENTS

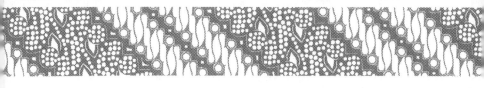

FOREWORD

August 2002: A thick fog began to descend upon the town of Sukabumi, West Java, blanketing the valleys between the surrounding mountains. That afternoon, about eighty top leaders of Bank NISP gathered at a resort called Javana Spa. When I arrived, I was greeted politely by a young man whom I later found out was the CEO of the bank. He introduced himself as Pramukti.

Pram, as I call him, invited me to be introduced to the ranks of his assistants. All of the people there were equally enthusiastic; the only difference among them was in age. What I noticed was that they were all young, except for a husband and wife pair sitting at the back of the meeting room. They were dignified and soft-spoken, and their kindness was reflected in their faces.

Later I came to know that that gentleman was Karmaka, whose name had been mentioned by several senior officers in the Economic Cabinet of Indonesia. Apparently, Karmaka was the source of energy that had kept this Indonesian private bank alive in its struggle to survive. He was the one who had sustained Bank NISP while overcoming a series of disastrous events and other predicaments over the last thirty years, before banking reforms were instituted. He was also the leader who had planted seeds of positive thinking and behavior, seeds that have flourished in his children and staff to this very day.

While I was giving the inspirational speech during the meeting that day, the husband and wife followed attentively. However, I noticed lines of sadness on their faces, and I thought that, whatever the cause of the sadness, it might be the reason why they chose to sit at the back. Several times I noticed Mrs. Karmaka wiping her eyes. At the end of the session, Karmaka apologized for not sitting in the front, saying that he needed to accompany his wife.

Later, I learned why. They had been in mourning for almost forty days over the loss of their eldest son, Pramana, a medical doctor, in an accident near the town of Subang. I could feel the sadness they bore. Several of the bank staff told me that a plan to postpone the meeting had been suggested, but the family had rejected it firmly, saying, "The meeting must go on!" I could sense they were saying, "Let us bear the burden of sadness alone."

The next day, I was still in the midst of the bank's activities, and my curiosity about the NISP family had not ceased. As a matter of fact, the bank at that time was still small. Its focus was on small businesses around the city of Bandung, but the bank had just declared its intention of becoming a national bank, serving the whole country. Its staff numbered around a thousand, and it had a limited number of branches in West Java. (NISP has six times that number at the time of this writing.)

Yet, my instinct told me that this bank would grow. I could tell by the values espoused by its leadership, that the bank had a bright future, and my prediction was proved correct. A year after the meeting, I was invited again to address the bank, this time on Bintan Island as part of the "Reaching for the Stars" program. In the span of only one year, the number of branches had grown 100 percent, and I saw new faces in management taking on new responsibilities.

Nonetheless, it was that first bright morning at the Javana Spa that would forever remain in my memory. That day, Karmaka narrated the long history of twists and turns in his health, intertwined with his struggle to save Bank NISP from a seemingly unending wave of disasters, some a result of the economic and political crises experienced by the nation at the threshold of the twenty-first century. Through all these times, Karmaka safeguarded and nourished the bank he had inherited from his father-in-law. However, the most intriguing story he told was about the liver transplant he had just undergone in the United States of America.

The incredible story of Karmaka is narrated in this book by someone who had had a similar liver transplant, Mr. Dahlan Iskan, the founder of the news agency, Jawa Pos.

Karmaka recounted the importance of keeping healthy. He did not miss a day of practicing Tai Chi, he said. And he did not merely go through the physical motions; he immersed himself in the spirit of the practice's healing effects. Karmaka said, "Legend has it that the emperors of China used to live only about forty years. A sage was called in to find a remedy. The sage then observed two long-lived animals, the crane and the turtle. From them, he devised exercises emulating the slow balanced feet of the crane, combined with the slow head and body turns of the turtle, and thus Tai Chi was born." From that point on, I understood the spirit of the act and the reason why Karmaka's life had been prolonged.

This book is the riveting story of a banker who has succeeded in his mission to create a business identity and culture that adapts with newer DNA, that of Karmaka's children, Pramukti, Rukita, Parwati, and Sanitri. All of them have their unique talents and yet complement each other to create a wonderful unity. From these stories, we understand the values Karmaka has instilled in them and why these values succeed, grow stronger, and remain eternal. The keys to success are in fact universal: Be honest, keep your good name, work hard, and dare to do what is right. We all know these, but not everybody is able or willing to practice them.

Enjoy the book, and my heartiest congratulations to Karmaka, to Pramukti and the family, to the people of NISP, as well as to Mr.

Dahlan Iskan

Dahlan Iskan, who has successfully preserved the story of Karmaka in a fascinating book that will inspire generations to come.

The House of Change, June 2008
Rhenald Kasali, PhD
Academic and business practitioner,
Professor of Management Science at the Faculty of Economics,
University of Indonesia

PROLOGUE: WHAT URGED ME TO WRITE

I became acquainted with Karmaka Surjaudaja three months after I had a liver transplant and two weeks after my best seller, *Liver Replacement*, came out. Karmaka flew from his hometown of Bandung in West Java to my city, Surabaya, in East Java. We met at the office of my publishing company, Graha Pena (The House of Pens). He told me that he had flown in for the sole purpose of meeting me and, with modesty, said that he wanted to have an exchange of experiences regarding my liver transplant.

It appeared that he had read my book, *Liver Replacement*. Even though he said "exchange of experiences," I got the sense that his real purpose was to advise me on how to take good care of myself. Karmaka gave his advice earnestly; he seemed to speak from the heart and was emphatic in the body language he used to stress the many precautions that I should follow strictly. In fact, I found Karmaka to be a highly spirited, energetic, and very caring person. Karmaka appeared more concerned with my life-extending transplant than I did myself.

Yes, I know why: Karmaka had had a life-extending liver transplant himself, ten years before I did. He advised me not to catch the flu virus and to cut down on strenuous activities, along with many other things. He came all the way from Bandung to deliver these precautions after hearing that I had begun resuming the very active schedule I'd enjoyed before my transplant. "No way, *Pak* Dahlan. You can't do that," he said.

I remember well the expression on his face when he said that. I remember well how he emphasized his words. I remember clearly his animated gestures. The encounter that day became a riveting dialogue between two people with the same fate—that of carrying someone else's liver. The more the discussion developed, as we recounted the journeys of our lives from their beginnings to the present, the more embarrassed I felt. The struggles I had had and the suffering I had encountered during the founding of the Jawa Pos media group was nothing compared to what Karmaka had gone through in rescuing his bank from obliteration. My liver transplant experience was also nothing compared to Karmaka's, which was followed by the removal of his nonfunctioning left kidney and an eventual kidney transplant that replaced his failing right kidney.

All of a sudden, I felt wrong to have selfishly written a book recounting my own liver transplant, when the person in front of me had more dramatic stories to tell. This feeling of unfairness swelled within me, as I realized that the experiences of someone like Karmaka was unknown to the public, while my book was being read by a multitude of readers. I felt I was being dishonest with myself.

On impulse, I offered to write Karmaka's memoir, and he immediately responded positively. This meant that an additional task would be added to my busy workload. However, Karmaka's struggles to revive an ailing bank, the bank's subsequent up-and-down fortunes, and its eventual prominence in the world of banking in Indonesia and South East Asia made for an emotionally captivating story indeed. The tortuous process for Karmaka to obtain his Indonesian citizenship, his positioning of himself as an ethnic minority who is concerned with the welfare of the majority, and his role in creating a tightly knit family are also compelling.

The appealing richness of the memoir's "raw materials" made me eager to write. While writing, I did not feel that I was at work; on the contrary, I felt as if I were watching a movie, captivated by feelings of joy, sadness, frustration, and anger at every twist and turn of Karmaka's life, followed by, finally, a feeling of relief.

Perhaps it was Pramukti, Kamaka's son, who first alerted Karmaka to *Liver Transplant*. After reading the book, Karmaka asked Pramukti to go with him to see me. In fact, I know Pramukti and his younger sister, Parwati, quite well from when they were president and deputy president of Bank NISP. I am also acquainted with their younger siblings, who were sitting on the bank's board of commissioners.

I feel grateful for the opportunity to know Karmaka deeply, to understand his personality and to learn the details of his life story, which helped to establish a trust and camaraderie between the two of us, as well as with his immediate and extended family. I have had the privilege of unearthing Karmaka's character; I have discovered his courage and tenacity in the face of the physical, mental, and spiritual adversities that have befallen him; his compassion toward his fellow human beings, regardless of ranks and riches; his vigor in confronting his enemies; his strong sense of fair play; and finally, his firm faith in the Almighty.

Jakarta, June 2009
Dahlan Iskan, Author
Chairman/CEO,
The Jawa Pos Group, Indonesia

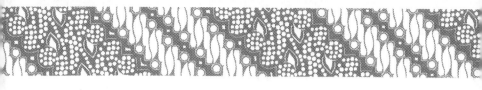

CHAPTER ONE

BLOOD, SWEAT, AND TEARS

As Karmaka Surjaudaja considers the many highlights of his seventy-four years on this earth, one stands out for him—witnessing NISP's transformation into one of the most prominent banks in Indonesia.

Why is that?

By almost all accounts, the bank founded by his father-in-law, Lim Khe-Tjie, should have been torn apart. It should have been utterly destroyed. If it were a boat, there were simply too many storms that should have drowned it. But incredibly, each time the boat started to sink, Karmaka was able to get it back afloat. Then, through some miracle he was able to fix the engine again. Eventually, by adding more "fuel"—his blood, sweat, and tears—he succeeded in getting NISP back on course to become the success it is today.

Anyone would be amazed and delighted to see NISP, after a long, torturous journey grow from a small local bank, limited to West Java only and ranked below fiftieth, to one of the Big Ten banks of Indonesia, with more than 360 branches, five hundred of its own ATM machines, more than a million customers, and assets of US $3 billion, as of 2008.

1

But Karmaka's happiness is multiplied many more times by this one fact; the current leadership of Bank NISP is comprised of none other than his own children, Pramukti and Parwati. This young generation has implemented its own initiatives to successfully establish new foundations for the growth, development, and modernization of the bank.

Karmaka feels blessed that he has been able to do good deeds in his lifetime. While he was battling the unceasing storms against NISP to ensure its survival, he could still guide and prepare his children so as to become the foundation of the bank in the future. Eventually, his plan and his efforts proved successful.

Karmaka is also filled with delight and pride to see his children leading NISP to new places. He never dreamed that, at seventy-four, he would see the NISP flag rise to the peak it has reached today. Moreover, Karmaka is still able to participate by visiting the bank branches and advising his children, who are now at the helm.

It is a miracle that Karmaka should be here at all. He should not have witnessed all these accomplishments. Karmaka should not have lived on this earth for so long. He should have died and been buried a long time ago. Several times, people tried to murder him. He himself attempted to commit suicide. He has been admitted to hospitals multiple times, undergoing several minor and major surgeries and, more than once, falling into a coma. Also, Karmaka suffered mentally when faced with seemingly unsolvable predicaments that threatened to render Bank NISP extinct, situations that arose not through any fault of his own, but as a result of circumstances and fate. Each time, he would suffer the mental and emotional stresses that came with having to take extreme measures, like laying off thousands of loyal employees and comrades-in-arms during the struggles to save the bank.

Karmaka often asked himself why, when one crisis was overcome, other crises relentlessly followed behind. And yet, no matter how thorny the problems he faced, how much his mental and physical capabilities to cope were exhausted, or how grave his near-fatal illnesses became, as if by some miracle, someone or some circumstance would offer him a way out and a solution.

Of course, by the time Karmaka reached his seventies, NISP had grown into a strong bank. As if by a miracle, Karmaka was indeed destined to see NISP's success. He considers this a gift from God to a person who, in his lifetime, was willing to work hard, be fair to others, use his wits and skills as best he could, and repent for his mistakes and sins. He is forthcoming about the remorse he has felt because of certain actions he took and decisions he made along the way.

Karmaka believes that, when all said and done, God was good to him. He and his wife, who has been steadfastly at his side through all the challenges he's faced, were destined to see their children, under their guidance, achieve success. The children who joined the bank, as well as the one who became a civil servant, all excelled, and Karmaka and his wife are proud of all of them. "I can see with my own eyes everything they've accomplished," says Karmaka.

In spite of being saved by good people from several murder attempts and his attempted suicide, death still threatened him. In 1996, Karmaka was given a death sentence. "One very famous liver specialist in the United States determined that I had been diagnosed too late with a terminal liver disease," he recalls.

Karmaka did his best and used all the means at his disposal to find a treatment. He traveled to the best hospitals in this world, but everyone he met told him he was past saving.

The only sliver of hope was to get a liver transplant. But Karmaka didn't want a transplant. At that time, liver transplantation was still an experimental surgical procedure, and the risks associated with the procedure were very high. "I rejected the idea. I would rather die in Bandung," he remembers.

But as his liver deteriorated and his wife and children continued to insist forcefully, he relented and had a liver transplant, which proved to be successful beyond even the expectations of the experts. That liver has functioned well to this day. However, five years after the liver transplant came another pronouncement of death. The doctor discovered that Karmaka had a severe kidney disease. There came a point when his kidneys were functioning so poorly that Karmaka fell into a coma. "Every one thought that I would die soon. They even prepared my portrait for the funeral," said Karmaka, laughing. At that time, Karmaka's children flew him, still unconscious, abroad to be saved. Karmaka was not aware of any of these events. Later, Karmaka agreed to have the worse of his two kidneys surgically removed, since cancerous cells had been discovered, and not long after, his remaining kidney deteriorated and was, ultimately, replaced with a kidney transplant.

"I, who was once arrogant before God, eventually came to admit the greatness and the blessings of God. He kept me alive after my suicide attempt and after the pronouncement of death from the two doctors for my fatal diseases. He saved me. Even after I was readied for my funeral, He gave me more years to live," Karmaka says.

"And that was not all that God did." Karmaka had faced three murder attempts, but God the all-knowing recognized who the evil ones were and took Karmaka's side. "Apparently, I was favored to live," Karmaka says.

Karmaka said that he was blessed to be saved many times from death so that he could see the result of his many sacrifices, his good intentions, his dedication, and his remorse for his mistakes.

"It seems I have also been given the chance to tell my life's story to all of you. Who knows, it could be useful as a comparison to another's life." He explains that he will tell me the candid story of the problems that almost sank NISP; he will talk about how he overcame the many problems that came his way, how he countered the threats he received, why he decided to commit suicide, and who helped to save NISP.

"I will also tell you how I had to face serious illnesses and overcame them one by one, how and why I prepared my children, how crucial my wife's role was, and how I feel now, after all the major problems have been overcome and I can see NISP prosperous and growing under the leadership of a third generation, since the founding of the bank on April 4, 1941, sixty years ago!" Karmaka concludes.

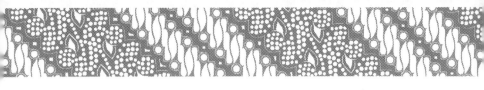

CHAPTER TWO

THE BABY IN THE SHIP

It was 1935, and the Chinese New Year celebrations had just ended. A mother and her ten-month-old son left their home village of Hokjia in Fujian Province in southern China and traveled to the port city of Xiamen (Amoy). The mother had decided that, once the New Year was over, they would follow the path of many others before them—they would *xia nanyang* (go down to the southern seas); in other words, they would immigrate to the hope-filled lands of Southeast Asia. The mother's destination was a faraway land that was later to become Indonesia.[1]

The mother sailed to this faraway land for the sole purpose of following her husband, Kwee Tjie-Kui, who had left the village in Hokjia two years earlier. Since his arrival in Indonesia in 1933, Kwee Tjie-Kui had lived in the city of Bandung, situated in the western part of the island of Java.

---

[1] The phrase *xia nanyang* describes the immigration of the Chinese to the promised lands in Southeast Asia. At that time, the countries of the region that we know today, such as Indonesia and Malaysia, had not yet been founded; most Southeast Asian lands were under European colonial rule.

The mother never talked in much detail about the journey that took more than ten days, except for the fact that the baby was fussy throughout the whole time. The sea gales, which were normally strong in February, would indeed have made the journey very uncomfortable, especially for a mother caring for a ten-month-old baby.

Just before the ship neared its destination, the port of Sunda Kelapa, now Jakarta, the baby came down with a serious illness—diarrhea. The baby's temperature was abnormally high. Because of the diarrhea, mother and child were refused entry, even though her husband was already at the port for the long-awaited reunion. The Dutch authorities refused entry for anyone with diarrhea and fever, for fear of epidemics. Mother and child were detained in the ship docked at the port for days. The father pleaded with the authorities for leniency but failed to move them.

Several prominent members of the Hokjia had accompanied the welcoming party from Bandung, and they also made efforts to convince the authorities to allow the mother and baby to disembark but with no success. Seeing that all efforts had failed, the father made the heart-wrenching decision to have his wife and baby return to Hokjia on the next available ship. He himself would accompany them and return to their old village in Hokjia, China.

But what if the baby did not recover from his illness, or worse still, were to die during the journey? With much anguish, the husband and wife came to the conclusion that they would have to live with the consequences, including the possibility of sea burial, though leaving the body of the baby at sea seemed unthinkable. There seemed to be no other way out.

In the midst of such desperation, Mr. The Tjie-Tjoen, the most prominent person in the Bandung Hokjia community, came to the rescue. He had been Kwee Tjie-Kui's guarantor when Kwee had first arrived in Indonesia. He tried to negotiate with the Dutch authorities and offered a higher amount of guarantee money—500 Dutch guldens, which was a large sum of money. The effort succeeded; the mother and sick baby were allowed to disembark and to continue the journey to their final destination, the city of Bandung.

In Bandung, the baby, who was named Kwee Tjie-Hui, gradually recovered and grew up healthy. The years passed, and when he was thirty-two years of age, Kwee Tjie-Hui became a naturalized Indonesian citizen and changed his name to *Karmaka Surjaudaja.*

"Yes, that's the only story of my childhood that my mother would tell me," says Karmaka, reminiscing about the fantastic beginning of his life's journey. "Mother never revealed the suffering she went through then," he adds.

Karmaka's mother remembered well the name of the big ship carrying her with the baby; it was the *Siliwangi,* indicating that this name had been popular even during the Dutch colonization. The name Siliwangi was given to king Sri Baduga Maharaja of the Pajajaran Kingdom in West Java, a tenth-century kingdom that existed long before the colonization of the land by the Dutch East Indies Company.

Karmaka's mother set out on her journey in accordance with a long-held Chinese tradition of embarking on a significant change in one's life right after New Year's Day. As to why his father made the journey ahead of his family, Karmaka explained that it was because his father was the headmaster of a school in Hokjia.

It is characteristic of Chinese communities, wherever they are, to give priority to the education of their children. The Hokjia community in Bandung was planning to set up its own school for the community's children. At that time, in 1933, the only available schooling in the land was in the Dutch educational system, but the Dutch authorities did allow the Chinese communities to establish their own schools. In Bandung, the Chinese wanted to establish a quality school; thus they needed to import the best teachers from China.

"At that time, Father was asked to come to Bandung to be the headmaster of the school," said Karmaka, recalling his father's story.

Kwee Tjie-Kui was attracted by the offer, which was better than the meager pay he earned for the same job in China. Furthermore, the request to move to Bandung came from a person of Hokjia provincial origin, someone who was famous for his very successful businesses in Bandung. This was Mr. The Tjie-Tjoen, the very person who would later put up the large sum to guarantee Kwee's wife and baby Karmaka when they arrived. "To come to Bandung, my father left behind my mother, who was pregnant with me. Therefore my father did not witness my birth," says Karmaka. "He was already in Bandung."

"The importance of education is also the reason that my elder brother, who was then three years old, was left behind in Hokjia, China, in the care of my grandmother's family," says Karmaka. "It was customary then for school-age children to be left behind for the sake of education. When I was fifteen, we got news that my older brother in China had died at the young age of seventeen, which of course meant that I would never have the chance to meet him."

At the time that Karmaka's father was appointed school headmaster, there was already a Chinese school in Bandung, but it was of a different Chinese provincial origin. The Hokjia community wanted to establish its own school, named Xin-hua Xiao-xue (New Chinese Elementary School) located on Gardujati Road. Years later, the Hokjia school system would expand to include middle and high schools, established at a larger complex on Cihampelas Road, at the northern outskirts of Bandung.[2]

Karmaka could not know very much about the pain of immigrating, since he was only ten months old at the time. Nor, when he was an adult, could he get much from his parents, who were reluctant to talk about the past. But based on scanty information and a few

---

[2] In 1966, the Communist party of Indonesia launched a coup-d'état, abducting and killing seven army generals. They were quickly subdued. Since the Chinese educational system seemed to be in sympathy with the Communist cause, all Chinese schools were closed and the properties were converted into state schools.

remembrances, Karmaka gathered that, upon arrival in Bandung, the family was given lodging with other newcomers in makeshift housing at a coffee processing factory in the Kebonjati area.

What Karmaka remembered was that his father was headmaster for about five years in the Xin-hua School. After that, when Karmaka was three years old, a younger brother was born, and the family moved to the town of Cibeureum, near the larger town of Cimindi along the main road leading to Bandung. A textile factory had hired his father to be its director of operations in the town of Cibeureum.

"My father was a hard worker. The factory owner was impressed by this and asked my father to change jobs and move there," says Karmaka. The move to the big new textile factory job would be accompanied by an increase in salary. Karmaka's father accepted the job since he had to take care of a growing family—his wife and two sons in Bandung, as well as the son who'd stayed behind in Hokjia, China.

Young Karmaka (right) with parents and siblings

CHAPTER THREE

THE GIFT OF FIFTY CENTS

After Karmaka's father accepted the position of director of operations at the facility in Cibeureum, the whole family moved to the little town at the western outskirts of Bandung. The family lived within the factory compound itself.

Karmaka was supposed to attend kindergarten at that age, but there was none in the town of Cibeureum, and going to Bandung for schooling would have been impossible. Commuting between Cibeuruem and Bandung would have cost a lot of money without a motorized vehicle in those days. "If I had gone to a Bandung kindergarten, I would have had to ride a horse cart every day, which would have taken about an hour each way and would have cost a lot," Karmaka explains. "Therefore, I was homeschooled for kindergarten, and my mother was the teacher." As a result, Karmaka attended neither kindergarten nor first grade at a formal elementary school.

Even though school took place in the home, the quality of the education Karmaka received was equal to or better than that of a regular school because Karmaka's mother had been an elementary school teacher in Hokjia, China, before emigrating. When she arrived in Bandung, however, she did not teach in a school there. She taught

Karmaka for three years and, later, taught his younger brother too. If he were in a regular elementary school, he would have been in second grade by the time the home schooling situation came to an end.

Yet, Karmaka longed to attend regular school with other children of the same age. Such a wish would not be realized until his father had worked for three years in the factory. The factory owner appreciated how hard Karmaka's father was working and so gave him a rental house in which to live. The house was at Hotel Homan Road No. 6, right in the center of Bandung itself. Karmaka remembered distinctly the day of the move and his delight that his wish to attend a regular school would finally and miraculously come true.

When he arrived at his new school, Long-hua Elementary School (he attended Long-hua rather than the Hokija community school where his father had been headmaster because of Long-hua's proximity to his home, which allowed him to walk), his homeschooling proved to be of high quality. After Karmaka took the required tests, he was placed in third grade, skipping grades one and two.

Karmaka first attended regular school in 1942, and it was the eve of the Japanese invasion of Southeast Asia during the Second World War. Before the school year was over, Bandung was occupied by the Japanese. The school stayed opened, but education was dictated by the occupying government. The assigned principal was under the watch of the Japanese ministry, the Japanese language had to be taught in school, and school discipline was in accordance with the Japanese norm. First thing each morning, the children conducted *Rajio taisō*—radio calisthenics—after singing the Japanese anthem while raising the Japanese flag. Karmaka studied the Japanese language seriously and always placed second in language competitions. (Mastering Japanese would later prove to be a valuable asset.) But who placed first in the competitions? Karmaka's younger brother. "He was smarter than I, but I have never felt jealous of him," Karmaka says. "As a matter of fact, I felt proud of him and proud of us two brothers monopolizing the Japanese language prizes."

Although he savored the prestige of being the best in Japanese, Karmaka found the climate suddenly changed. When he was in fifth grade, Japan surrendered unconditionally to the Allied Forces, ending the Second World War. Suddenly, the long-suppressed yearning of Indonesians to be free from colonization exploded. Independence movement leaders Sukarno and Mohamad Hatta declared Indonesian independence on Friday, August 17, 1945, seventeen days before the signing of the Japanese surrender on the battleship *Missouri* in Tokyo Bay. As was to be expected, the Dutch government did not recognize the declaration.

Bandung was split by a railroad running east to west, which separated the Allied temporary governing body in the north from the freedom fighters in the south. The freedom fighters launched a guerilla campaign, and Bandung was one of the strategic cities being contested. The Dutch plan was to retake the southern part of Bandung; therefore, the freedom fighters were forced to burn the southern part of the city to prevent the Dutch from reoccupying it. This event, dubbed "Bandung Sea of Fire," was featured in the song, "Hello, Hello, Bandung." This patriotic anthem, which is still sung to this day, describes the heroic struggles of the freedom fighters against recolonization and ends with the exhortation, "Now Bandung burns like a sea of fire; comrades, let's take it back!"

Karmaka's family was very much affected by this battle. Desperate to stop the freedom fighters, the Dutch occupiers in the north opened the sluice gates of a huge reservoir in Curug Dago's northern hills, the source of the river Cikapundung. Water rushed into the main river, the Cikapundung, which passed through the center of the city and flooded large areas of the south. Karmaka's house, at Hotel Homan Road, was in the path of the flood. The flood destroyed the yard and the lower part of the house and almost drowned Karmaka's family of five (another brother had been born).

"We were trapped in the house for three days and three nights," Karmaka remembers. "We couldn't leave the house or make contact with anyone, and there was soon no more water left to drink or food to eat."

His mother took a piece of white cloth, tied it up to a pole, and started waving the white flag through the window. She shouted for help, as the family was at risk of drowning and starvation. His father did not dare to emerge, for there was a warning that any adult males on the street would be shot. The situation was very tense. On the one hand, the Dutch kept up the attacks against the guerillas, and on the other, the Japanese, who had not completely surrendered their weapons, continued to use Hotel Homan as a headquarters. From the upper floors of the hotel, the Japanese troops could see the house and could shoot any male coming out from it.

On the third day of the flood, his mother's efforts finally brought results. The Japanese soldiers recognized the family's plight and allowed the family to emerge from the house. Karmaka and the family immediately came out. Karmaka walked while his two younger brothers were carried by their mother and father. "My father said we needed to evacuate and go to a safer place," Karmaka remembers.

But where was there to go? "North! Anywhere, as long as it's north, where it's safer," shouted Karmaka's father.

The family walked along Bandung's most opulent street, Braga Road. When they had almost reached the railroad tracks that served as the border between north and south Bandung, they heard someone calling. With delight, the family recognized Mrs. Xip Ping-Xiang, the owner of the Hong Kong Restaurant. "The restaurant owner pitied us, a family in dirty and tattered clothing with nowhere to go," recalls Karmaka.

The Allied occupational forces recovered the south but were still surrounded by the freedom fighters at the outskirts of the city. In spite of tensions and skirmishes between the conflicting parties, the Hong Kong Restaurant remained in business. The customers were mostly

Dutch and other Europeans from the Allied Forces. Some normalcy returned to the family's life, as the five resided for free in the restaurant basement, helping with the cooking and dishwashing in return. They ate mostly leftovers from serving the customers. "Even though we were eating leftovers, we felt very happy," says Karmaka.

The living quarters in the basement, which was close to the Cikapundung River, were used as a storage place. The place was infested by ants, mice, lizards, and other creepy creatures. Karmaka and his two younger brothers were delighted to catch and play with these creatures, and because of the experience, Karmaka would never be disgusted by small creatures.

Even though they lived on handouts, Karmaka's mother never stopped striving to earn her own living. After her restaurant duties were over, she found time to bake cakes and cookies, and Karmaka and his next younger brother peddled the wares along luxurious Braga Street and the surrounding houses. They had to sell all the cakes; otherwise, their mother would be very angry and they would be punished physically. This experience so affected Karmaka that later in life, he was ready to endure any hardship and not to shrink from facing any adverse circumstances.

One day, Karmaka's next younger brother received a big gift. An English family with children came to eat at the restaurant. During the meal, one of the customer's children dropped and scattered toys all over the floor. Karmaka and his brother quickly crawled under the table, retrieved, and cleaned the toys. The guest was very pleased with the help and, knowing the brothers to be poor, asked Karmaka to order two servings of fried rice for Karmaka's family.

At that moment Karmaka's smart brother, who was standing behind him, started yelling, "No! No! Money! Money," meaning that he would like to have money instead of fried rice.

"I was so angry at my brother," Karmaka remembers, "that I whacked his foot with mine, and I heard his loud 'OUCH.'"

The English customer, admiring Karmaka's impeccable character, smiled at him said, "Well, well, well," and handed Karmaka five dimes (fifty cents).

Karmaka inspected the coins closely, thinking *Wow! It really is five dimes.* The usual tip was five cents. His brother immediately tried to grab the money from Karmaka's hand, thinking that his begging had worked. Karmaka held on to the coins and suggested a plan; they would keep the money secret from their mother, and if they weren't able to sell all the cookies, they would enjoy eating them and make up the money from the Englishman's gift.

Karmaka (left) with younger brother,
Kwee Tjie Ong

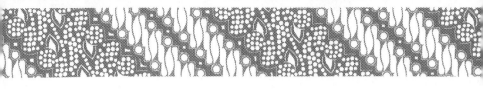

CHAPTER FOUR

DROPPING OUT OF SCHOOL

At the peak of Karmaka's enthusiasm for schooling, his father broke his back in a serious accident at the textile factory. Even though his father was the director, once in a while, he lent a hand when labor was short. He was helping to move drums of chemicals for dying colored cloths when he was injured. "They were 100-kilogram drums, and my father was not strong enough to handle them," Karmaka explains. "Even the doctor said that it would take a long time for the wound to heal for full recovery enabling him to work again."

At that time, Karmaka was in his second year of middle school at Hua-Qiao Zhong-Xue. But now the family had lost its breadwinner. In those years, there were no job security regulations for businesses allowing for sick leave. Where would the money come from for school fees for himself and his younger brother, not to mention household expenses? Moreover, the family had, by then, two additional brothers to feed and care for. Karmaka, as the eldest son, knew what he had to do. He would stop going to school and start working.

Given his father's good reputation, the textile factory offered Karmaka a job in the dye mixing area. His main task was to inspect the quantities of incoming materials and the correct usage of chemical dyes for cloth coloring. Karmaka worked very hard to prove that he could work as well as, if not better than, a mature worker. He was only fifteen years old at the time.

One day, the owner of the factory, accompanied by the plant manager, made an inspection of the plant. When the pair came to the chemical dye mixing area, the owner saw the very young worker and asked the manager, "Who is this boy?"

"He is Kwee Tjie-Kui's son," said the manager.

Immediately the boss told the manager to move Karmaka from the area, saying "Do you want to poison his lungs with these chemicals?"

Karmaka silently praised the owner, delighted to find someone who cared for a young worker like him. The mixing room reeked of chemical vapors, which the workers, including Karmaka, breathed in. At that time, there were no regulations to speak of to assure the workers' safety.

Karmaka was immediately reassigned to the administrative office. Young Karmaka thought his fate would be better working in an office, a much cleaner place. However, this was not to be the case. The manager, now angered by the boss having treated a common worker with such special care, decided to make Karmaka's life miserable. He assigned Karmaka to typing letters. "I know his intentions were not good," says Karmaka, remembering the start of his misery. "I had never learned to type well and made a lot of mistakes." From the manager's unfriendly facial expression, Karmaka sensed that the manager was up to something when he said, "When typing a letter you cannot make *any* mistakes!"

That first day of typing, before even one sentence was completed, he mistyped a single letter. He discarded the letter and started all over again, but then he made another mistake. At that point, the manager shouted at Karmaka: "You're *stupid*! You are stupider than a buffalo[3]!" The manager jabbed Karmaka's forehead with his index finger, pushing him off balance, a very humiliating gesture in Indonesian custom.

---

[3]   an Indonesian idiom

The manager shouted, "You have ruined two sheets of paper; for that, you have to pay! Your salary will be cut for these!" The words about a cut salary sounded like thunder booming in Karmaka's ears, shaking his nerves, and stabbing his heart. The humiliation and threats hurt Karmaka to the bottom of his soul. He wanted to cry for someone to help him, but at the same time, he wanted to explode in fury at the manager's face.

But Karmaka kept silent and endured. He could not bear the thought of losing his job and jeopardizing the livelihood of his family. At the moment of enduring his agony, Karmaka was determined not to forget it and made an oath to himself: *I will not be humiliated anymore in my life. I will strive to work hard. I must succeed. I will be better than this cruel manager. When I am successful, I will not be cruel to anyone. I will help the poor.*

To this day, Karmaka can still feel the pain and vividly recalls the manager's name, his facial expression, and his gestures, as clearly as if the cruel manager were in front of him right now. Yet, being ethical, he has never revealed the manager's name in public.

Meanwhile, Karmaka was coping with a very real and frustrating question: how was he going to become successful without going back to school and finishing middle school?

Luckily, Karmaka worked in the textile factory for only one year. His father's back injury eventually healed, and he went back to work in the same textile factory. Karmaka was so delighted to go back to school like other happy youngsters, enjoying normal youthful lives. Moreover, driven by vengeful feelings toward the factory's cruel manager, he resolved to study hard and achieve the highest grades in every class.

Enthusiastically, Karmaka registered again at his previous school after one year of absence. Learning that he had to start all over from the level he had left, which meant that he was one year behind his younger brother, was a blow to his enthusiasm.

"Never mind," said Karmaka, "I am going to catch up to him!"

Karmaka (front row, second from left) high school years.

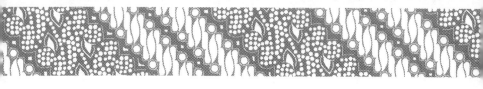

CHAPTER FIVE

DREAMS ON HOLD

Putting his schooling on hold for a year in order to work in the textile factory wasn't the only sacrifice Karmaka made for his family.

"I longed to attend the premier Bandung Institute of Technology to study electrical engineering. I had a fondness for anything electronic. I was sure to graduate cum laude and become an electronic engineer," said Karmaka, recalling his youthful dreams. However, no matter how much he was enamored by electronics, no matter how certain he was to graduate from a premier university with accolades, and no matter how often he dreamt that he would be an electronic engineer, he was confronted with the reality of his life; he was the eldest son of many siblings in a family with meager resources. In the Chinese tradition, the eldest son must bear the burden of the family's responsibility and be an example for his siblings in his willingness to sacrifice for the welfare of the family. Even though Karmaka was too young to be imposed with such heavy responsibilities as having to work at such young age, he successfully finished his schooling and graduated high school at the same time as his younger brother.

Having two sons graduating from high school at the same time posed a financial burden to the family; it would be costly to send both boys to college. Karmaka's younger brother, Kwee Tjie-Ong, wanted to study at the country's premier medical school, the University of Indonesia, which was located in Jakarta, the capital city of Indonesia 150 miles away from their hometown of Bandung. Kwee Tjie-Ong knew that Karmaka wanted to study electronic engineering at Bandung Institute of Technology (Institut Teknologi Bandung, ITB) and that Karmaka had taken night classes in electronics during high school of his own accord. As a matter of fact, Karmaka was so serious about studying electronics that he had gotten his diploma early, and the owner of an electronic repair store promptly offered him a position at the store. Each day after school, Karmaka worked in the radio repair shop, a place where he could indulge his hobby and earn money for his future studies at the Bandung Institute of Technology.

One morning, Kwee Tjie-Kui summoned Karmaka and Kwee Tjie-Ong. He explained that because of the family's limited resources, only one of them could attend college. The other had to sacrifice his dreams and find work to support the one getting the higher education. "I saw my father weeping as he said those words. I was shocked to see tears streaming down his cheeks," Karmaka recalls.

Karmaka pondered deeply over the dilemma. Eventually, he came to a decision—he would sacrifice, as this was the best course to take. This strength of character and willingness to sacrifice for others would be evident again later in his life.

"Let Tjie-Ong go to medical school and let me work," he said.

"No, no. I'll go to work, and you go study electronic engineering," replied his younger brother.

Upon hearing that, Karmaka affectionately hugged his brother and said to him, "Don't do that. One of us has to be successful; you have to be a doctor. We have been humiliated for too long for being poor. You study hard and become a doctor for the pride of the family". His younger brother, weeping, hugged him tighter and replied, "No, brother, it will take me too long to become a doctor, and more than ten years to be a specialist. It will be quicker for you to become an electronic engineer."

Karmaka was resolute; his younger brother would attend medical school at the prestigious University of Indonesia. And as the eldest son of a Chinese family, Karmaka had veto power over his younger siblings. He said to Tjie-Ong, "I am truly willing to let you be the one to go to university, on the condition that you quickly become a medical doctor and an excellent one at that." Karmaka was confident that his brother would make it, knowing that his brother was smarter than he.

Having been vetoed, Tjie-Ong replied, "All right, I promise that I will study hard. When I am a practicing doctor, I will pay for your studies in electronic engineering at Bandung Institute of Technology, even if you are married and have children of your own at that time".

Even after conceding the opportunity to attend college, Karmaka's desire to attend ITB was never completely extinguished. His first thought was to get a scholarship or a loan to pay the tuition. He would then find a job that would allow him time to attend the classes. For such an arrangement, he made contacts with all potential donors and lenders. He approached people in the Chinese community, especially those who knew his father well. "It failed," Karmaka recalls. "Nobody was willing to give me a scholarship."

He then thought of another plan. He would earn money while pursuing his interest in electronics; he would open an electronics repair shop.

Coincidentally, the owner of the electronics shop where Karmaka had worked after school was feeling too old to continue with the business. He told Karmaka that he would gladly sell it to him. The owner thought that Karmaka would be the best person to take over.

"I remember very well the amount he asked for the business—30,000 rupiah!" says Karmaka. "When I worked there, my pay was 5 to 10 Rupiah per night. The 30,000 rupiah was only for goodwill and inventories. There would also be rental and utility expenses," adds Karmaka.

But the allure was too strong for him. So once again he visited the people to whom he had appealed for his college scholarship. Once again, his requests for a loan, this time to buy a business, were not successful. "I was looked down on because of my age and my lack of experience. They didn't believe I could repay the loan," Karmaka explains. "Besides, nobody would bank on a poor family like us."

Still, Karmaka did not give up. He was hoping that the kind owner of the textile factory where his father had worked and where he himself had been a miserable dye mixer and typist might be convinced to give him a loan for the electronics shop. With great reluctance, Karmaka visited the factory. But as luck would have it, he was received by the very manager who had humiliated him and made him miserable when he was working there. The manager had since been promoted to deputy director of the factory. Not to be deterred, Karmaka toughened himself up and asked for the help.

Just like before, Karmaka was assaulted with a torrent of insults. "You do *not* know who you are! You are nothing but a poor beggar! Moreover, your father still owes us money that has not been paid back! Who do you think you are asking for a loan?!" yelled the manager.

Karmaka's dream of sitting in the lecture room of ITB faded away. His goal to own and run a small electronics shop had vaporized. He had to begin working so that he could earn a living and support his family, including covering the cost of tuition and board for his younger brother for his medical studies. What job could he find?

One of the Chinese schools, Nan-Hua Xue-Xiao, happened to be searching for a physical education teacher. Karmaka immediately took the job and became a teacher who was well liked by the students. He was also a highly valued member of the school due to his talent in a variety of sports. However, the salary was too meager to support the family. To supplement his income, he began tutoring students from well–to-do families at their homes during the evening hours.

As time passed, Karmaka's hard work allowed him to provide for the family financially and to support his brother's studies. Furthermore, he was very proud of his brother's excellent grades and that Kwee Tjie-Ong had completed his studies on time. Karmaka was very happy. His dream of having a family member attain success had come true. Family pride was boosted by the fact that, very soon, a member of the family would be a practicing medical doctor! To have a doctor in the family was a sign of prestige in the society of the time.

But then, like a bolt of lightning, devastating news arrived from Jakarta. Kwee Tjie-Ong had passed away in a traffic accident right after graduation, just when he was getting ready to specialize in internal medicine.

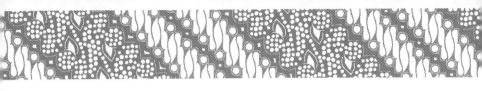

CHAPTER SIX

MORNING TEACHER, AFTERNOON WORKER, EVENING TUTOR

Although Karmaka had worked at both the textile factory and the radio repair shop, teaching was his first career. His position as a physical education teacher at Nan-Hua Xue-Xiao was his first permanent position, and the job was a good match for him. He enjoyed athletics and was good at them.

"Even though I was only 1.65 meters tall, I could jump over a 1.75 meter bar," he recalls. "I was third in the high jump in the Bandung Chinese High Schools' field & track competition."

Nan-Hua was delighted to have Karmaka on its staff. Aside from his work as a physical education teacher, he helped solve school problems. For example, Nan-Hua could not afford a sound system for broadcasting announcements to each classroom. With the help of friends, Karmaka scrounged for electronic parts in electrical junk stores and assembled a sound system. Also, as someone who was handy and liked to tinker, he was also able to improvise the necessary athletic equipment for his track-and-field classes.

Karmaka's athletic skills were not limited to the high jump. He was good at discus and javelin throwing and all kinds of gymnastics.

For example, he could hold different styles of handstands for twenty minutes or more. These exercises, which required physical discipline and endurance, surely helped him gain the stamina and fortitude he would display in the face of incredible mental and physical challenges throughout his later life.

However, the immediate challenge that he could not defeat was his meager salary of 600 rupiah per month. This was not enough to pay for household expenses, including feeding the family, which had grown nine children by the time.

"I needed more income," he said. "I kept trying to figure out what else I could do, but it was not easy to find another job." The school recognized his hardship but was helpless since the school's income from tuition was less than what it needed to pay even the teachers' salaries. To overcome the deficit, the school used progressive school fees; that is, well-to-do parents paid higher tuition to compensate for the lower fees from those who were poorer. Another source of income was the yearly funding campaigns targeting individuals and businesses donors in the Chinese community.

Confronted by his inadequate income, Karmaka's heart was divided. He should find another job with higher pay, but then he would have to relinquish the teaching job that he loved and enjoyed so much.

One of the school trustees knew of Karmaka's problem. He informed Karmaka that his friend, the owner of a big textile company, might have a job for him. "The boss is a very kind person and is well respected in Bandung community," the trustee told Karmaka.

Karmaka followed up the lead by visiting the company and meeting with the owner. At the end of the interview, Karmaka was truly shocked. "I was immediately hired at a salary of 1,800 rupiah a month," he said. "That was three times my 600 rupiah per month teaching salary!" Without hesitation, he decided to take the job and, without saying it, he vowed to do his best and work hard to dedicate himself to the prosperity of the company. "The company owner had entrusted me with such a high salary. I could not let him down," added

Karmaka. Later, Karmaka would make good on his silent promise, uncovering inefficiencies and irregularities that would turn things around and improve the company's profitability.

The immediate issue, however, was Nan Hua could not relinquish a valuable teacher like him. Karmaka was very well liked by both students and fellow teachers. Likewise, Karmaka himself found it hard to abandon a rewarding profession. He enjoyed witnessing the fruits of his and his fellow teachers' enthusiastic and concerted efforts, as students became better people. He was also reluctant to give up teaching athletics and tinkering with electronics.

Fortunately, he reached a compromise. Karmaka would teach from 6:00 to 8:00 a.m. before going to the textile factory and again after work from 4:00 to 6:00 p.m. In between his split teaching shifts, he would work six hours in the factory from 9:00 a.m. to 3:00 p.m. The factory owner's great concern for the welfare of the community made this arrangement possible; he wished to see the Nan Hua School succeed.

Karmaka's involvement in athletics in his youth would have significant impact later in his life when he would promote sports in the cities of Bandung and West Java. As the new owner of Bank NISP, he would pay special attention to sports, even assigning one of his sons to establish and coach the National Softball Team of Indonesia, which won the Regional Tournament of 1990. The first coach of the team was Karmaka's first son, Pramana Surjaudaja, who was a medical doctor and MBA holder.

In spite of his twelve-hour-a-day workload, Karmaka still found time to earn more money during the evening hours. Since Karmaka was seen as a very good teacher, he was in great demand by well-to-do families to tutor their children at home in the evening in mathematics, physics, chemistry, biology, and other natural sciences. Therefore, after a long day's work, Karmaka extended his work by three more hours in the evening, working from 7:00 until 10 p.m. as an evening home tutor.

Among the many families he served as a tutor in the evenings was a very special one—the lives of this family's members would intertwine with his own. One of the daughters of this family would become his partner for life.

Karmaka (second row from top, rightmost) with fellow teachers.

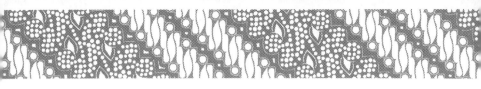

CHAPTER SEVEN

INCREASING EFFICIENCY AND UNCOVERING WASTE AND THEFT

The owner of the company tasked Karmaka with a very important job—to increase manufacturing productivity and business profitability. These tasks were critical to the success of the company due to the increasing competition in the textile business at that time. Whoever was most efficient and, thus, most profitable would win the race.

To accomplish these tasks, Karmaka began conducting an inspection of the manufacturing processes. He studied every step of the operations, often lingering in one place to carefully observe and analyze what was going on. He did this throughout the entire operation, starting from the raw materials and working his way to the finished product—a variety of merchandized cloths.

He would often work extra hours, staying late on Saturdays when the plant would close early, at one o'clock, and coming into work on Sundays in order to inspect the operations that needed to be running continuously seven days a week. He did all of this voluntarily, expecting no overtime compensation for the extra hours. He wanted to show the owner that he was dedicated to his job as an appreciation for the owner's trust in him and the salary he was receiving. Working without overtime pay, he felt, was nothing compared to the owner's generosity in pay and leniency in allowing him to set his own work hours so that he could continue to be a physical education teacher at Nan Hua.

Karmaka concentrated first on the cloth-weaving section. There, he found quite a few workers who seemed "lazy." "I often saw workers who were half awake and inattentive in running the weaving machines," recalled Karmaka. Consequently, when a string of yarn broke, the worker did not notice it until yards of substandard cloth were produced. Because these cloths were defective, they had to be discarded as scraps. Karmaka thought that whenever a string of yarn broke, the operator should immediately stop the machine, dismantle it, and correct the cause of the break. Since yarn was the main raw material in the manufacturing process, the more yarn the company could save, the higher the profit would be for the company.

At that time, weaving machines were not equipped with yarn break detectors that automatically stop the machine. Therefore, workers' attentiveness was critical, particularly in the operation of semi-manual machines. The weaving machines were rated to produce two meters of cloth per hour without yarn breaks. Karmaka analyzed past operation data with regard to yarn breaks. The results were appalling. Cloth defects due to inattentiveness were as high as 8 percent, much higher than the industry average of 1.5 percent.

How would Karmaka solve this problem? "I tried to become closer to the workers," he remembered. He assembled all the workers in the weaving department and talked to them in a friendly manner. "I want you all to realize that if we do not pay attention to the operations, the company will become less competitive in the market. If that were to happen, the company would have to be shut down, and your livelihoods would be in jeopardy."

After the speech, Karmaka pondered over what actions should be taken. He would rather implement an incentive system to reward workers when the number of defects was low than one to penalize poorly performing workers. Karmaka calculated that if defects could be reduced from 8 percent to 4 percent, productivity would increase by 2 percent, which would, in turn, increase profitability by 2 percent. If defects could be further reduced to 2 percent, then the incremental profit could be used for a workers' welfare fund. In addition to creating the incentive of a workers' welfare fund, Karmaka devised a bonus for those whose work had the least amount of defects.

"I presented my idea along with the analysis to the management. The company owner agreed to the incentive plans and asked me to implement the systems on a two-month trial basis," said Karmaka. Karmaka presented the plan to the workers, who embraced the incentive systems enthusiastically. At the end of the two-month trial, Karmaka collected and analyzed the data and wrote a report. The results? "Very satisfactory!" said Karmaka. "I cannot remember the exact amount of how much money we saved, but it was substantial—so substantial that the boss was very pleased and impressed!"

Next, Karmaka launched an investigation focusing on irregularities in the consumption of diesel oil used to run the plant's steam boiler. The oil consumption of the boiler was too high, almost double what was specified for that model. At first, Karmaka thought that the feed valve opening was incorrectly set or that, perhaps, a worn-out valve needed replacement. Upon inspection, however, the valve opening was set correctly, and there was nothing wrong with the valve device itself. From a technical standpoint, the boiler should have been consuming less oil than what the purchase manifests showed.

If Karmaka had not been more diligent than the other workers, coming in to work on weekends, the oil wastage problem would have never been uncovered. Karmaka discovered several things that made him suspicious. First, the oil deliveries were almost always on Sundays when few people were around, and oil wastage jumped up during delivery days. Since Karmaka often came to work on Sundays, he used the occasion to watch the oil delivery procedure. Second, the oil delivery truck driver's assistant would always go to the warehouse manager, who was responsible for receiving deliveries, and the manager appeared to give something to the assistant to be delivered to the driver. However, Karmaka could not accuse anyone without clear evidence of foul play. "I needed to pull a string buried under a pile of powder without scattering the pile," Karmaka explains.

One Sunday, Karmaka casually walked over to the driver and greeted him by handing him two sticks of cigarettes, an Indonesian custom. Noticing that the driver seemed a bit moody, Karmaka asked, "Are you sick?"

"No, sir, but my wife is," the driver replied. "We don't have money to buy medicine."

To Karmaka, the driver's reply was a fortuitous opening. He gave the driver 5 rupiah, a delightfully large sum. Week after week, Karmaka would chat with the driver and give him little gifts until Karmaka had earned the driver's trust. Eventually, the driver told him how the oil was stolen. The tank was loaded fully as indicated by recorded, metered amount in the purchase manifest; however, at the bottom of the tank, a partition prevented complete drainage.

Karmaka was surprised by the way the oil was stolen. He calculated the loss to the company caused by the cheating that had occurred throughout the whole year. The warehouse manager had stolen a painfully large sum of money.

Not intending to curry favor from the factory owner but purely out of concern for the company's profitability, Karmaka immediately reported his findings to the owner. His report included the financial losses that had been ongoing for who knows how many years. At that point, Karmaka expected the owner to be glad that a large loss had been uncovered. Alas, the outcome turned out to be a disaster for Karmaka. Upon receiving the report, the owner became tremendously enraged, and he blasted the warehouse manager with the foulest language he could think of. The owner was furious that his subordinate had blatantly deceived him.

Nevertheless, the warehouse manager maintained his position. In those days, most companies were family owned, and it was obligatory that all critical positions were held by members of the extended family. In this case, the warehouse manager was a close relative of the company's owner.

As a result, the warehouse manager hated and haunted Karmaka. Many annoying incidents began to happen. For example, at the end of the work day, he would discover that his bicycle was broken or had a flat tire. He would have to take it to a repair shop and wait for it to be fixed during the precious time he had before catching up with his teaching job at Nan Hua. "I often did not have the time to rest and snack between jobs because it was taken by bike repair," recalled Karmaka. He kept all these annoyances to himself. He did not want to complain to the owner, for fear of complicating the issue since the warehouse manager was the owner's relative.

The factory owner, having been saved from wastage and cheating, paid a lot of attention to Karmaka. He was impressed by Karmaka's dedication, self-confidence, astuteness, and honesty and wanted to retain Karmaka forever. He made Karmaka a fantastic offer. He would provide Karmaka with a car and a house, as well promote Karmaka to be one of the company's directors. This offer came with one condition that would tie Karmaka to the company forever.

For a young person whose sole mode of transportation was a bicycle, the offer was beyond belief. Karmaka was shocked and confused, but even more so when he heard the condition of acceptance. It was something he did not expect at all: he was to be wedded to the daughter of the owner's relative.

A combination of shock, pride, delight, apprehension, and confusion swelled in Karmaka. Having his own house and a car would bring pride and delight; it would be a huge improvement from pedaling around in a bicycle. But being a director would make him nervous. He came to the conclusion that taking such a position would cause too much turmoil within the owner's extended family, especially after what had happened with the oil-cheating incident. Karmaka did not want to be the source of strife within the owner's family.

As for the condition of marriage, his answer was a simple "no." "Though I am tempted by the house, car, and high position within the company, I do not want to break my oath. I have promised my heart to someone else, and my heart belongs to her," concluded Karmaka.

CHAPTER EIGHT

KEEPING A PROMISE

At times, Karmaka could not help but ask himself, *Am I crazy to reject such a life-changing opportunity?* The promotion, house, and a car aside, marrying into the owner's family was an opportunity to lift his family from poverty.

By then, Karmaka's reputation for being hardworking, clever, and honest had spread among the textile manufacturing circle. Unexpectedly, while he was procrastinating on how to reply to the company's owner, another major textile company offered him a job that was no less enticing. This company was in the process of expanding and modernizing its operations. The offer included three years in Japan for training in modern textile technologies and business operations and a position as the head of operations in Jakarta.

The offer did not include material things such as a car and a house, but it was the very thing that Karmaka had been longing for. It would provide him with an opportunity for higher education. Though it was not Bandung Institute of Technology, studying overseas would be equally prestigious. "At long last, I have the chance to get an education beyond my high school diploma," he remembered saying to himself. As for the language, he was not too concerned as he had gotten second place in Japanese language competitions during elementary school. "It was as if I were in a dream," said Karmaka. He pondered the prospect. *Is this my path to studying at a university?* he asked himself. *Is this my reward for the sacrifices that I made for my family?*

Now he had a good reason (the opportunity to study in Japan) to reject the offers of the first company. Karmaka finalized his reply to the owner of the first company, who had been so kind to him. "At that time, I had planned exactly what I wanted to say to him and how I was going to say it. First, I would thank him for the generous offer of a high position and the marriage arrangement. Then, I would earnestly apologize for rejecting the offer," recalled Karmaka. In his heart, he had two reasons for the rejection. He declined the offer of marriage because he had already made a pledge to someone else, and he declined the offer of directorship in order to avoid the complicated extended family relationship he would be involved in if he were to be part of the company management.

What was the owner's reaction to Karmaka's rejection? "He was in shock!" said Karmaka. "I guess the owner could not believe that I would reject such alluring offers. He was assured that I would accept them, knowing that I had been bicycling from one job to the other," Karmaka said. It was also a very touching moment. "He was in tears. I did not know why. Was it from disappointment, frustration, or was he disheartened by my firm rejection?"

Karmaka had wondered what the company's owner would say, and he was surprised to see that the owner did not say a word. The owner was silent for a long while, as tears ran down his cheeks. Seeing his boss in tears, Karmaka was also silent, and then he also wept. Karmaka felt sad and very uneasy about being placed in such a predicament. However, he was resolute. He had to leave the company to pursue a higher ambition—studying abroad in Japan. A month after that emotional day, Karmaka left the company.

Karmaka then turned his attention to the offer the other company's owner had made. In his heart, Karmaka felt ready to fly to Japan. He met the boss several times to discuss the preparations for the journey and schooling. In the beginning, the discussions went smoothly, but as time went on, something made Karmaka feel uneasy. The company's owner began talking about one of his close relatives who had a daughter who was studying abroad. Eventually, it came to be known that he planned to have this young girl be wedded to Karmaka.

This talk of wedding was another shock to Karmaka. He could not believe that he was being thrown into another intractable situation. He knew that, to most people, such a circumstance would not pose a problem; on the contrary, they might even welcome it. However, to Karmaka, the situation was problematic because he had already pledged his heart to a girl that he loved. He had been teaching her at Nan Hua and tutoring her at her home in the evening.

Once again, Karmaka was faced with another choice—between the highly tempting offer of a university education in Japan, along with running a modern textile company, and the commitment that he had made to his sweetheart.

In the end, Karmaka was resolute; he rejected the offer from the second textile company. He did it with tact and respect toward the owner of the second company. Karmaka knew very well the risk that he took by rejecting the offer. It rendered him practically jobless. He could not go back to his old job; nor could he support his family by making teaching his long-term career. He had found himself in all of these quandaries because of one reason—keeping the promise he made to his sweetheart.

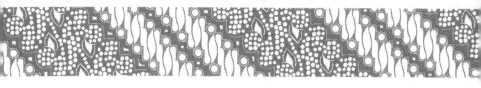

CHAPTER NINE

SWEETHEARTS

Who was this lady who had captured Karmaka's heart so strongly that the penniless young man would reject two very alluring offers? He was moved by neither a car and a house nor a directorship. The offer of studying abroad and leading a new, modern textile company could not tempt him. This lady had to hold a very special place in the twenty-four-year-old's heart.

"I have been in love with her since the moment we met when she was a student at Nan Hua Middle School. At that time I was the physical education teacher," said Karmaka. "That was the first time I had ever fallen in love, the first time that I had a feeling of adoration hitting me with such intensity. Her name was Lim Kwei-Ing."

Apparently, Lim Kwei-Ing found herself falling in love with Karmaka in turn. She saw in him a very responsible young man who was full of energy. She was impressed by the roles he held at Nan Hua. Not only was he the physical education teacher, he also, of his own accord, assumed other responsibilities for the betterment of the school and expected nothing in return. Kwei-Ing knew well that Karmaka was from a poor family, but that did not prevent her from falling in love with him. She herself came from a very rich family. In fact, her father was one the wealthiest and well-respected businessmen in Bandung. Every day, Kwei-Ing came to and left from school in a luxurious car, a rarity in those days.

In contrast, Karmaka arrived at school riding the old bicycle that he'd inherited from his father—the key to his ability to support his family by doing arduous tasks. Kwei-Ing knew about Karmaka's busy schedule, pedaling between the school and the textile factory and back and finally to the houses of rich families to tutor their children. She knew that, oftentimes, when problems needed solving in the textile factory, Karmaka would have to rush back to school without lunch. She would frequently bring food for him, either buying it or bringing it from home.

Karmaka saw in Kwei-Ing a woman with good character and integrity. Even though she was born to one of the wealthiest families in Bandung, she worked hard to complete her chores in the house. She was not spoiled, as most rich children were. If she were spoiled, marriage to a husband with meager resources would be complicated. Karmaka was well aware of the Chinese tradition that a man should bear full responsibility for the welfare of his wife and not be dependent on his wife's family's fortune. "I did not expect to see Kwei-Ing doing housework," said Karmaka. "But she did it with dedication, and I never heard her complain. She happily and enthusiastically completed her tasks."

Apparently, Kwei-Ing's parents had an interest in and even hope for Karmaka. In 1958, they sat Karmaka down to talk to him. Kwei-Ing's father, Lim Khe-Tjie, expressed his wish to visit his place of origin in China. It is the tradition of Chinese emigrants that, after they become successful abroad, they pay homage to their ancestors by visiting and cleaning the graves of their ancestors. The Chinese believe that when deceased ancestors are well treated, they will reciprocate by safeguarding and bringing fortune to their descendants left on earth. Lim Khe-Tjie was very successful; he had become one of the richest men in Bandung with a thriving business. He also owned a well-respected bank and had just established another bank. However, he had never visited his ancestors' cemetery in Hokjia village since leaving China and sailing the South China Seas to Indonesia as a poor, penniless man. "Before I leave, I want Kwei-Ing to get married," Lim Khe-Tjie said to Karmaka, and he asked Karmaka if he would be her husband.

Lim Khe-Tjie knew well that the couple had fallen in love with each other. He was fully aware that Karmaka came from a poor family. However, he was not worried as he saw in Karmaka a hardworking young man with a strong sense of responsibility.

Yet, Karmaka thought it was too early to get married. He felt he had nothing to offer for a decent marriage, and on top of that, he was responsible for supporting his own family. He thought that he should not get married until he was thirty years old.

Karmaka told Kwei-Ing that he loved her and would marry her. He proved to her that he was committed to her as evidenced by his rejections of two marriage offers that would have given him wealth, a career, and educational advancement. But to marry right now? He had never thought of marrying so soon.

Karmaka asked Kwei-Ing to have a serious discussion with him. Swallowing back the difficulty of speaking these words, he asked her if she would regret being married to a poor family such as his own. "I don't have a house. I even have to borrow a bicycle from my father. I have to support the schooling of my nine sisters and brothers," Karmaka challenged. "We will live miserably. Won't you regret that?"

Kwei-Ing understood the circumstances she faced and the risks she would be taking. Calmly, she answered that she was ready and willing to live together with Karmaka in spite of all the risks. She said that she was willing to struggle in order to fulfill the needs of her new marriage. Besides, she was accustomed to working hard at home. Kwei-Ing was fully confident that she would have a happy life with Karmaka, whom she knew to be a kind-hearted and highly responsible person.

Her resolute commitment was music to Karmaka's ears; he felt exalted and moved. The young couple fell into each other's arms, hugging each other passionately.

It was not until almost a year later that the marriage was realized. The wedding ceremony was held in the building of the Bandung Hokjia Association. The reception, an unusual event due to Lim Khe-Tjie's well-connected and well-respected position in the community, was attended by more than a thousand guests. Karmaka and Kwei-Ing were dressed in Western style clothing, not in traditional Chinese wedding clothing. However, the ceremony itself was conducted according to the ancient Chinese wedding rituals.

After the wedding, Karmaka brought his new bride to his parents' residence at Hotel Homan Road. There they began their humble life together in a less than well-to-do household among Karmaka's nine younger siblings.

Karmaka and Lelarati, newly wed.

Wedding day, 1959, Karmaka's parents (left) and Lelarati's parents (right).

CHAPTER TEN

LEARNING HOW TO SERVE
AND BE WISE

Karmaka found himself at once married to the girl of his dreams and jobless. Without the very good job in the textile company he had relied on, his responsibilities—to provide for himself and his new wife while remaining the financial backbone of his family, financing the education of his younger brothers and sisters—seemed daunting.

Lim Khe-Tjie knew that his son-in-law was out of work, except for his part-time jobs as a school teacher and tutor. Seeing how desperate his son-in-law was for work, he introduced Karmaka to one of his acquaintances, the owner of Padasuka Company, a textile manufacturing and marketing business. Mr. Tan Lin-Tjik was known in the community as one of the kings of the textile industry, as well as a patriotic hero. He had been involved in Indonesia's fight for independence from the Dutch during the Dutch attempt to recolonize Indonesia after the Japanese handed over to the allied occupation forces at the end of World War II.

The community of Bandung and its surroundings respected Tan Lin-Tjik, and the government of West Java held him in high regard. The leaders of the independence movement recognized his contribution during the guerilla warfare against the Dutch. He had provided supplies and ammunition to the independence fighters and given refuge to them in his factories when the Dutch forces pursued them.

Karmaka was sent to work in a factory in a small farming town called Majalaya, located at the southern outskirts of Bandung. At that time, there was no public transportation between Bandung and Majalaya. Therefore, every morning at 5:00 a.m., Karmaka walked to the city center, a green field surrounded by government buildings, a mosque, shops, and two movie houses. He would stand in front of the Radio City movie house to wait for the military trucks that would give people rides for free since military trucks regularly passed through Majalaya. Karmaka would prepare two cigarettes for the driver, along with words of gratitude. Arriving in Majalaya, the truck stopped by the main road, and Karmaka walked the remaining few kilometers to reach the factory.

Even though he worked every day and did not get home until nine o'clock at night, Karmaka was very happy with his work at Padasuka Company. "I felt very fortunate to be under the wing of a well known and respected boss, Mr. Tan Lin-Tjik. He was a very influential person in the world of business and was very skillful in getting along with people and adept at communication," Karmaka remembered. "I really learned a lot from him."

Several weeks after Karmaka began working in Padasuka Company, his father-in-law finally departed for China to fulfill the Chinese tradition of "cleaning the graves" of the ancestors for good fortune. He took his whole family except for Kwei-Ing, Karmaka's newly wedded wife, with him.

Since the factory was located in Majalaya, communication among the managers and workers was mostly conducted in the West Javan dialect, Sundanese[4]. Tan Lin-Tjik himself was very fluent in Sundanese

---

[4]   The official language of Indonesia was the Malay language, which originated from the peninsula of Malaya. Historically, the Malay merchants in the archipelago spread their language, and it functioned as a common language for communication among people with different

and conversed with ease, which facilitated his close friendship with the leaders and elders of the local community, such as Haji Rahmat and Raden Soemantri. These elders often invited Karmaka for lunch, which was usually in a bamboo constructed "tea house" near a refreshingly cool fish pond. The young man learned a lot from those elders, in addition to having the chance to practice his Sundanese, since he was brought up speaking the regional Chinese dialect of Hokkian.

Karmaka worked for Tan Lin-Tjik in Majalaya for a few years, but he never got involved in or knew about his father-in-law's many businesses, including the bank. Karmaka was not aware of these businesses, as he had never been given any tasks to manage or monitor any of them. According to the old Chinese tradition held at that time, the family fortune was shared with the extended family only through patriarchal lines. Because he was wedded to Lim Khe-Tjie's daughter, Karmaka was excluded from her father's family business.

Karmaka focused on his work in Padasuka Company and enjoyed it very much. He would long cherish his friendships with the owners and community elders, who still hold a special place in his heart. Years later, the son of Mr. Raden Soemantri would work diligently and enthusiastically for Karmaka's Bank NISP. Mr. Tan Lin-Tjik would eventually pass away, and his children would continue the business. Furthermore, Padasuka Company, which had always been a good customer of Bank NISP, would continue this relationship.

Karmaka worked hard for Padasuka Company for five years. He would literally work from dawn to dusk, often getting home late at night. His experience at Padasuka taught him a lot; among the lessons he learned were how to build human relationships, how to serve people well, and how to be a wise man.

This knowledge and experience would soon serve him well, as his father-in-law was about to give him a very difficult mission.

---

ethnic languages. Language-wise, the island of Java is split in two; the western third, where Bandung is located, speaks Sundanese, while the eastern two thirds speaks Javanese.

The Surjaudaja family in year 1976

The children, from left to right:
Parwati, Rukita, Pramukti, Pramana, and front, Sanitri

CHAPTER ELEVEN

A CALL TO SAVE THE BANK

Karmaka did not know about the serious problems Bank NISP faced. At the time, while Karmaka was working at the Majalaya textile factory, several staff members from the bank came to see him. These bank workers asked Karmaka to help save his father-in-law's bank. Some of Karmaka's visitors even recounted NISP's problems with tears in their eyes.

But Karmaka could not respond to their requests. He had not been given the task to manage or monitor the bank by his father-in-law. As a son-in-law, Karmaka did not want to be seen as having an interest in his in-law's businesses without an invitation. He assumed that his father-in-law knew about the problem anyway. So, he continued to focus on his job at Padasuka Textile Company.

However, the bank's situation was getting worse, and its employees felt uncertain about their future. So, they kept approaching Karmaka about saving the bank. They reminded him that, even without orders, it was only appropriate for a good son-in-law to help save the bank owned by his father-in-law.

The staff told Karmaka that not long after his father-in-law had gone to China to pay homage at his parents' graves, some of the bank management had made a systematic attempt to gain control of Bank NISP by making themselves minority shareholders, and had embarked in speculation. Karmaka's father-in-law was being betrayed by people he trusted; in the meantime, he was unable to come back to Indonesia to confront the betrayers.

It was not until 1962, when Karmaka had been with Padasuka Company for almost four years, that his father-in-law called from Hong Kong. Anger clearly tinting his tone, Lim Khe-Tjie asked Karmaka to save the bank. Karmaka was surprised at his father-in-law's raw, clear emotions. Lim Khe-Tjie had trusted the people who now threatened his business for a very long time.

"You get into Bank NISP!" Lim Khe-Tjie said. "You have to take over the management!" His tone quieted as he offered his son-in-law guidance. "Don't give your trust away to people too easily. People are basically good by nature, but greed can turn anyone bad." He told Karmaka at length about his employees' disloyalty. "All of them got together to betray me," he explained with great disappointment. "I gave them free shares in the company so that they would be more responsible in leading and growing the business. How could they have done this to me?!"

His father-in-law gave him names, but Karmaka did not reveal them to anyone. Knowing the names of the disloyal employees helped him to recognize who the enemy was, and he was ready to address the core of the problems.

On the other side, the bank staff continued pressuring Karmaka to immediately save Bank NISP. The staff was worried about the fate of the bank, as well as their own futures. "Before too long, we could lose our jobs and our livelihoods," said one staff member.

Now that Karmaka had a direct order from his father-in-law, he was ready to face the challenge. He immediately looked for a way to skillfully and safely insert himself into the management of the bank. As a complete stranger to bank management, Karmaka thought hard about what he had to achieve. He fully realized that he did not know what banking was all about or how to run a bank. He also realized that he had only a high school degree, and worse, he was not an Indonesian but a Chinese citizen.[5] According to regulations, he had to be an Indonesian citizen to be a bank director. His only assets were a quick mind, a strong sense of responsibility, a fighting spirit, and his mastery of the Sundanese language.

Day and night Karmaka thought hard about the best way to get into the bank management. If he made a mistake, he would certainly fail and be ridiculed as a fool who wanted to lead the bank. Karmaka could not stop thinking about what to do. "I felt a strong sense of responsibility," he says. "If I failed to carry out the tasks given me by my father-in-law, how could I face my wife's family?"

Meanwhile, Karmaka's wife bolstered him. "Why hesitate?" Kwei-Ing said.

Karmaka listed all his weaknesses and all the difficulties he would face. Banking was an arena he knew little about, and the ramifications of any misstep would be serious.

But Kwei-Ing knew what her husband was like and what he was capable of. "Don't hesitate! You have to think that it is possible, and

---

5   Throughout history, the Chinese government has claimed all Chinese and their descendents who have migrated overseas to be its subjects, thus granting them full citizenship. The colonial Dutch government in Indonesia granted Chinese migrants and their descendents full residency. When the Republic of Indonesia was established after the Second World War, all Chinese born in Indonesia were granted full citizenship in the Republic of Indonesia. This dual citizenship issue was settled by an agreement between the Republic of Indonesia and the People's Republic of China in 1955, in which any Chinese of age eighteen and older, including his or her children, had the right to refuse the automatic granting of Indonesian citizenship. Since Karmaka was born in China, he had to apply through naturalization to obtain an Indonesian citizenship.

then it *will* be possible," she pressed. "I know you're always ready to work hard and you always rise to challenges. You can definitely do it!

"This is a valuable chance to prove to my father that you can do it," she added. "An opportunity like this one doesn't come twice."

Immediately Karmaka's heart settled, bearing a sense of responsibly; he would prove his worth to his wife's family.

CHAPTER TWELVE

FRAUDULENCE IN THE BANK

The fraudulent activities taking place within Bank NISP while Lim Khe-Tjie was in China paying homage to his ancestors' grave might never have been discovered if they had been on a smaller scale. Khe-Tjie might never have known about the trouble had it not involved the interests of the bank's customers, who started complaining directly to him. And Lim Khe-Tjie would not have been angry if his reputation with the public, and in particular with his customers and relations, had not been tainted.

The serious fraud carried out by some of the bank's managers had reached the point where it was sullying Lim Keh-Tjie's name and causing his clients to lose trust in him. In Hong Kong, Khe-Tjie heard report after report that his name was the subject of scorn and rebuke. Khe-Tjie was accused of running away with his customers' money. "Of course, my father-in-law was in an immense rage. He had been one of the most trusted and respected people in Bandung. It was because of his impeccable reputation that NISP Bank was so trusted by its customers and was able to grow so rapidly," said Karmaka.

Lim Khe-Tjie could not bear to see his good reputation ruined. One could gain wealth, but a person carried his or her reputation to the grave. "If the problem cannot be solved, the bank fails, my name is ruined, and I will not be able to close my eyes even if I die," Lim Khe-Tjie said. When Karmaka heard this, he felt the weight of responsibility to solve the problem even heavier upon him.

Lim Khe-Tjie continued to hear reports that many NISP customers were withdrawing their deposits. This by itself was a danger. The bank would fail if deposits were withdrawn continuously. The customers not only withdrew their money, they added angry words. "We were cheated by NISP!" they shouted.

What had happened? How were the customers cheated? The problems began with an enticing promotion the bank had offered its wealthy customers two years earlier. In 1960, the year after Lim Khe-Tjie left Indonesia, NISP offered any customer who was willing to deposit 1.8 million rupiah in cash into his or her account, a used Impala brand car would be delivered in a reasonably short time.

At that time, cars were considered luxury goods. Car imports were strictly regulated, and quantities were limited. Only certain merchants holding special licenses were able to import cars. The Impala brand was a status symbol, and wealthy people were anxious to own an Impala. However, even someone who had the money might not be able to buy an Impala because of strict import quotas. At that time, the country had a low foreign exchange reserve for importation of goods.

The car promotion was extremely attractive. Even people who did not want to own a car were tempted to hand over the 1.8 million rupiah so that they could turn around and resell the car for a large profit. At that time, you could ask as much as 4 million rupiah for a used Impala, and a long line of people would be waiting to buy it.

Three thousand bank customers ordered an Impala through NISP's promotional offer! And why not? For a mere 1.8 million rupiah, a customer could get an Impala and double his or her money in a short time!

Apparently, some people from the bank's management, people who Lim Khe-Tjie trusted, had established an export-import trading company. It was their private company, but they used the NISP name. It was that company, and not Bank NISP, that was pretending to import the Impalas.

The owners of the export-import company never used the money they collected from bank customers to import cars; instead they invested it in a very high-risk business—rubber commodity trading, which was very hot in the international market at the time. The embezzlers plunged into the rubber market for the tantalizing possibility of high returns. They fantasized that they would achieve a huge windfall profit from the rubber trade exporting to Malaysia and Singapore. Then, they would use part of the profit to buy the Impala cars, as if rowing a boat to two treasure islands and sweeping up the bounties all at once.

But the rubber-trading treasure island was not an island of gold after all. The island was full of treacherous reefs and poisonous fish. The embezzlers completely failed at the rubber trade, beaten by more experienced people from other countries. Consequently, the money that was supposed to be used to import Impalas was totally wiped out; not a cent was left.

The customers who had been eagerly anticipating the Impalas started asking questions. The delivery times had been rescheduled over and over again. At the beginning, the customers were not too suspicious because they trusted the NISP name and the reputation of its primary owner, Lim Khe-Tjie. But after many delays, rumors began to circulate about fraud in the bank. Finally, after almost a year, the customers, who had been very patient, got angry. They criticized NISP and condemned Lim Khe-Tjie. They began to penalize the bank by using a tactic guaranteed to frighten any bank—withdrawing their money.

Lim Khe-Tjie heard the threatening news, but he was powerless. He could not return to Indonesia because, for some reason, his Indonesian passport had become invalid. Furthermore, he did not know whom he could still trust. He had not been able to be involved in the daily operations of the bank he owned for three years.

Karmaka never speculated about who suggested that he be appointed to save the bank. "Maybe it was my father-in-law's own idea," he says.

Unfortunately, as it turned out, the Impala case was not the only case of fraud. It was soon revealed that the culprits in management, in fact, owned several other businesses. Using these businesses, they'd borrowed money from Bank NISP. They never paid back many of the loans; nor did they keep the interest payments up. Furthermore, when collateral of bad loans were liquidated, the malefactors arranged things so that the bank suffered losses instead of retrieving the loans.

Such practices were rampant in the banking business at the time. Management, sometimes even in collusion with a bank's owner, would fail to record transactions, mark fictitious credits, and engage in other such fraudulent practices. One such scam allowed bankers to steal customer deposits. A customer would make a deposit, and the transaction would not be recorded, allowing the funds to be used outside the bank. The customer would receive a seemingly legal, signed certificate of deposit. If the bank failed, the customer could not claim the deposit since the regulators could not find such a transaction in the books. At that time, it was so difficult for a bank owner to control the management that some owners chose to share ownership with managers or seek other options or grants to reduce such risks of fraudulence.

Such extremely irregular practices would be very difficult to pull off in modern banking systems. If bank managers did try to implement these scams, they would likely be discovered before large amounts of money could be swindled. But this was in the 1960s; anything could happen. Therefore, in those days, the owners would generally roll up their sleeves and directly control the bank, keeping an eye on management processes. Departments such as credits, deposit receiver, and cashier usually had to be controlled by the owners themselves or by their most trusted relatives. This was especially true of the position of cashier; holding this position was a sign that management trusted you highly.

When Karmaka was trying to enter the bank's structure, he thought he could start by holding the lowest and simplest position—that of cashier. Of course his request was flatly rejected!

CHAPTER THIRTEEN

YOU REAP WHAT YOU SOW

How would Karmaka join the bank? He had never been acquainted with the people managing the bank; nor had he even entered the bank building at all.

As a first step, he met the president of the board directly. He remembers the event well. Just as he has never forgotten the time when he was insulted and ridiculed by the deputy director of the textile factory, the words the president of the board and the executive president threw at that meeting would ring in his ears for years, even decades.

In the meeting, Karmaka expressed, in the most polite way, his father-in-law's wish for him to participate in the management of the bank. He did not say a single word about his father-in-law being angry, as he did not want to upset the manager in his first attempt to work his way in. "My father-in-law asked me to help solve the challenges faced by the bank," Karmaka told them.

Karmaka was not surprised by the corrupt managers' answer, which was essentially a direct rejection of his request. Karmaka knew very well that his presence would wreck the schemes they had been running. "It is not possible for you to be part of the management team because you are not a college graduate," one of the threatened managers said.

Karmaka had already guessed that his educational level would be used against him. So, he was ready with other strategies—requests that wouldn't allow management to use his lack of college education as an excuse. Finally, he asked to be made a cashier, a position he assumed was low on the totem pole. Even though the position of cashier was not a high one, Karmaka realized it would open up a path for him to receive some important information related to the fraud, as he would have access to cashier records. Also, being a cashier would allow him to detect further fraud.

However, this request was also flatly rejected. The crooked managers recognized, of course, Karmaka's "door-key" strategy. Hearing Karmaka's request to become a cashier, the manager could not find a reason to reject the request. Therefore, he immediately used anger as his next tactic.

"I am offended!" said the dishonest manager, banging hard on the table. "Am I no longer trusted? Am I suspected of mismanaging the bank's money?" he demanded.

Karmaka backed off. He did not want to continue the tense meeting. *Of course you people are no longer to be trusted!* he thought to himself. But he kept his mouth shut.

It seemed he had not yet found the right door. But that was all right; visiting the bank and delivering a subtle message to the corrupt managers was his first step to finding a way in. In this first meeting, Karmaka had essentially given the dishonest managers a signal that there would be another round of fighting.

Knowing that Karmaka had come to the bank and talked to the managers, the employees believed that Karmaka would soon join the bank's management. What the employees did not know was that management was completely rejecting the wishes of the bank owner.

Karmaka discovered that many of the employees had little sympathy for management. These employees came to him and told him not to lose hope. They knew who had ruined the bank—the managers of the bank—and they felt they had been victimized along with the bank's customers.

The pressure on Karmaka from the employees grew more intense as the crisis worsened by the day. Many customers were filing suit in the state court. They asked the court to prosecute the bank and to seize and liquidate the bank's assets. The situation had reached the "red alert" state.

About twenty senior bank staff members finally offered Karmaka a suggestion. "Together we can go to the authorities," said one of the staff, speaking for the others. "We will also have to go to the court to request that the injunction and liquidation of bank properties be postponed."

The staff's thinking was that, if Karmaka could sit in management, Lim Khe-Tjie's good name could be used again. Karmaka would be "sold" as a family member who would represent Lim Khe-Tjie's interests. In that way, the customers could be convinced not to withdraw their money or sue NISP for the Impala car fiasco. In other words, Lim Khe-Tjie's good name could still be an assurance to the customers.

Finally, Karmaka agreed to appeal to the banking authority and to the state court. The staff told Karmaka the essence of NISP's trouble. "The problem is not with the bank, but with a situation created by minority shareholders who sit in the bank management. It has nothing to do with the bank business or its operations," a staffer assured him. This argument was to be used to convince the banking authority and the state court

In addition, the staff delegation requested that the authorities cancel the plan to close NISP. "If NISP falls, the biggest victims will be its customers, and because it is a savings bank, 90 percent of its customers are lower income people saving the little money they have," the delegation's spokesperson argued. The delegation furthermore petitioned the state court to return the already confiscated bank assets.

When all those tactics failed to fully convince the authority and the court, the staff delegation drew yet another weapon out of its sleeves. They used the "you reap what you sow" approach against the corrupt management. "If there must be a confiscation, the court should confiscate the personal assets of the fraudulent managers instead of the bank's assets," one of the delegates suggested.

Finally, the delegation offered an assurance that if the court agreed to cancel the confiscation of the bank's property, Lim Khe-Tjie's family, who were the controlling shareholders, would assume the responsibility of ultimate guarantor. These words of promise became important. Almost all the customers understood very well that none of Lim's family members sat in management positions; thus, the family was not the cause of the crisis NISP faced.

"This is the warranty; Mr. Karmaka Surjaudaja, Mr. Lim Khe-Tjie's son-in-law, will assume full responsibility on behalf of the interests of the controlling shareholders," the delegate told the banking authority. "Consequently," the delegate explained, "Karmaka should be given a seat in bank management."

Extraordinarily, the strategy Karmaka and the bank employees employed proved to be very effective. Moreover, their notion that the fraudulent managers must reap what they'd sowed became a viable tactic, ensuring that those who'd actually committed the fraud were cornered. Eventually, this case would receive a lot more exposure. The state court would appeal to the Supreme Court to settle the case, which by then had escalated as the court turned its focus away from bank failures and toward the illegality of the rubber export and the fraudulent promises of car importation.

The government cancelled the confiscation of NISP's assets. Instead, as the staff had hoped, the government confiscated and auctioned off the offenders' private property. This confiscated property included not only goods, houses, and lands, but also the bank shares that Lim Khe-Tjie had given to the managers a long time ago. Karmaka was surprised at the extent to which the percentage of the fraudulent managers' shares had grown. It seemed that, after Lim Khe-Tjie's departure, the managers had used unethical means to increase their ownership of shares, which at the time of confiscation had reached a high of 43 percent. The government confiscated the shares because the value of the remaining property was insufficient to repay the loss incurred by the three thousand customers who had ordered Impalas.

More than that, however, all the fraudulent managers were sent to jail.

But even after all of this had occurred, customers continued to withdraw their money from the bank. This, said the staff members, was because the bank did not have an effective means of convincing the customers to trust NISP. They needed something that would decrease the customers' emotional anxiety. They wanted to be able to tell their customers that Lim Khe-Tjie's family had come back and taken over NISP's management. However, they could not go ahead with such a statement because the banking authority had not approved Karmaka as a director in the bank.

He was still held back by two factors—his lack of a college degree and his citizenship status. Karmaka found himself constantly assuring both the staff and the banking authority that it was not his fault—that he had been applying for Indonesian citizenship through naturalization for many years.

Finally, the Bank of Indonesia, the country's reserve bank, accepted this reasoning and agreed that Karmaka could be the director of NISP, on one condition. He would obtain his citizenship by June 1, 1966. Otherwise, his directorship would be rescinded.

Even though the citizenship issue was not under Karmaka's control, he agreed to the condition. In fact, the deadline set by the authority offered welcome breathing room. With three years to go, Karmaka thought he could get citizenship by the proposed deadline. The most important thing was that NISP would recover and be back to normal operations before those three years had passed.

CHAPTER FOURTEEN

THE LABOR DAY SPEECH

Both the bank's board of directors and its board of supervisors[6] were shocked that the banking authority had approved Karmaka's request to become a director at the bank. They were very unhappy with the decision. They had already rejected Karmaka's request to fill a lower position, that of cashier, and now suddenly Karmaka was going to become a director. Karmaka didn't worry about them. He knew that the majority of the workers and staff members supported him and were, in fact, happy with the decision.

However, in order to implement the banking authority's decision, a shareholders' meeting had to be called. Calling a shareholders' meeting was not easy, as most directors and supervisors were working to block Karmaka's appointment. Karmaka finally used the services of a lawyer, who was a close friend of his father-in-law. "He was a very good person and did not want to be paid," said Karmaka. "He said he just wanted to help my father-in-law and get NISP back on its feet again. I marveled at this gentleman and was really touched by his kindness," said Karmaka.

---

6   Indonesia's banking uses a two-tier system; the board of directors holds an executive role, and the board of supervisors oversees.

As the name shareholders' meeting indicates, Karmaka was going to meet face-to-face with the other shareholders, the people who disliked him the most. At the meeting, Karmaka acted as proxy for his wife, who had power of attorney for her father. Since Lim Khe-Tjie was still the majority shareholder, the outcome was inevitable; Karmaka was accepted as a new director of NISP. Furthermore, it was an appointment that the Bank of Indonesia had already approved and that the majority of the employees supported.

But even as a director, Karmaka's hands were still tied. The people associated with the swindlers remained as directors and commissioners, who could block or at least hinder any measures Karmaka took. But Karmaka felt glad and remained enthusiastic. "I was glad because this was a new challenge. This was a new experience," Karmaka explained.

Along with building momentum for change, Karmaka worked to calm customers, especially those who had paid for the Impalas. He visited those customers one by one, explaining the problem and convincing them to give him a chance to make amends. Some customers understood, and others remained very angry.

In his explanation to the customers, Karmaka had to explain that what had happened was the fault of certain individuals inside NISP and not the bank itself. He explained that these individuals had been apprehended and their property, including their bank shares, had been confiscated. These properties would be sold or auctioned off. It would take time for the process to play out, but Karmaka assured them that the value of the properties to be sold would be enough to pay back bank obligations to them.

With that approach, the customers became less inclined to withdraw their money. Indeed, people started once again to deposit their savings into the bank.

In addition, Karmaka immediately conducted an audit. The staff members enthusiastically helped him conduct the examination. Through the audit, Karmaka found clear evidence that the crooks had perpetrated extensive fraud. These criminals had made numerous questionable loans, loaning to companies they owned, approving loans without proper collateral, and maintaining loans with unpaid interest. Karmaka also discovered that the same individuals had improperly bought and sold many of the bank's assets.

Gradually, the audit findings became the talk of the employees. The employees were very upset to learn that, all along, their difficulties had been the direct result of these individuals' actions. Cases like this became a political target in the 1960s, when the left used terms such as *capitalist bureaucrats, bourgeoisie,* and *rotting capitalist* to attack all kinds of institutions, including corporations. Moreover, the fraud had created huge losses for the bank, which made the workers even angrier. To them, it was proof that workers were left to suffer while capitalist bureaucrats became rich and fat.

In workers' meetings, these sensitive issues were repeatedly brought up, especially as Labor Day approached. The situation was heating up, and NISP managers were becoming anxious as well, fearing they would be targets of protest in Labor Day mass meetings.

Their fears were soon realized. On Labor Day, the workers of NISP planned to conduct a huge rally. They invited the entire leadership of NISP, including Karmaka, who had been a director for just a few months. Karmaka, who did not really follow politics much, did not feel he had any issues with the workers.

Karmaka accepted the invitation of the bank labor union to attend the rally. He was puzzled and surprised when he saw no other NISP management present at the huge workers' rally. Some had claimed to be sick, while others said they were busy with other business. He found himself in the middle of a lot of workers who seemed to be very unhappy with management.

Soon Karmaka saw the leader of the labor union walk onto the stage. He saw that the man was a very skillful speaker, whose speech was forceful and full of emotion. This was the first time Karmaka had watched someone giving a political speech. In his strident voice, the leader expressed his disappointment that, at this important gathering, only one person represented management.

Karmaka would never forget the blistering words spoken that day. "See, my friends! Our managers are all fat! Their lives are prosperous!" the union leader shouted.

Karmaka felt a chill upon hearing those words. It was true that he was rather husky. He weighed 75 kg and stood only 165 centimeters, so he appeared fat.

Karmaka felt uneasy but could not do anything. He continued listening to the labor leader, who was, in fact, one of his employees.

"We, the workers are suffering! We are thin and bony! Exploited by the bank! Right?" shouted the leader from the podium.

"Rrrrright!!" shouted the crowd with the same gusto.

"We must demand justice!" the speaker shouted. "Where is justice? Is not that our right?"

Once again, the attendees responded enthusiastically.

Karmaka grew increasingly uncomfortable. He glanced left and right. "I did not know how to respond," remembers Karmaka. He also felt very upset because none of the other managers had come at all. He guessed they had purposefully left him there alone in a difficult corner, and he would have to find an exit by himself.

Then it dawned on him that he would likely be asked to give a speech. But he did not know how to make a speech and had never attended this kind of a meeting before. His guess turned out to be correct. The master of ceremonies explained that the next event would be greetings from the bank manager. There was no escape. Karmaka found that, willing or unwilling, able or not, brave or afraid, he *had* to step up to the podium.

Shaking, he approached the podium. "However, on the steps up to the podium, I became determined not to surrender to circumstances. I also did not want to be confrontational with the workers because there was no problem between them and myself. I had to be positive, to motivate them, and to gain support from them," recalls Karmaka.

Karmaka opened his speech with words of thanks for the invitation given to him for the event. He then continued by speaking about his new position, heading the bank in the last few months; he joked that, although he was fat, it was not from swindling the bank.

Surprisingly, Karmaka's attitude and honesty made the audience receptive to him and his speech. He told the truth about what had happened with the bank. "I can understand very well how you all feel," said Karmaka, to the applause of the audience.

Seeing the positive response, Karmaka became more enthusiastic and more sentences flowed out naturally, sentences that made the workers feel more thrilled. "Why do I understand your feelings? Because for twelve years I myself knew what it was like to be a worker. For eight years I worked in a textile factory, and for four years as a teacher," he said.

Again the audience applauded willingly.

Sensing support from the workers, Karmaka felt it was time to ask for something in return. He was going to use this positive situation to save the bank. If the workers took damaging actions against the bank, it would be difficult for the bank to recover. "However, my friends, you should know that the bank is facing a serious problem. Our bank is enduring a loss of trust from customers. Our business is at a critical moment," said Karmaka.

Hearing those words, the workers became silent. They were ready to listen attentively to the next words Karmaka would say.

"All these problems were the result of the actions of a few irresponsible individuals inside the bank," he stated. "Our bank is at the brink of bankruptcy."

Because of this precarious situation, Karmaka narrated, he had been asked by the bank owner, his father-in-law, to save the bank. "I was asked to work together with all of you to find a way to prevent the bank from falling into bankruptcy," said Karmaka. "My father-in-law values every one of you. Let us work hand in hand to protect and develop NISP. Be assured that if NISP becomes prosperous again, I guarantee I will pay attention to the welfare of the workers. All of us will prosper together," Karmaka stated firmly.

Karmaka felt relieved. He finished his welcoming speech and came down from the stage to enthusiastic greetings from the workers. Many of them even embraced Karmaka. Some even wept.

Karmaka was very moved. He had turned the ceremony, which initially seemed to be a trap, into a powerful weapon. "I will never forget that Labor Day," he says.

CHAPTER FIFTEEN

REMOVING THE TRAITORS

Backed by widespread support from bank staff and workers, Karmaka felt increasingly confident. Yet he remained very disturbed at the findings of the full audit; the extent of the corrupt managers' fraud was hard to stomach.

Karmaka decided that the best way to resolve the situation was to reorganize the bank's management structure. To be exact, he needed to get rid of those who had betrayed his father-in-law's trust.

Since Karmaka was already a bank director, he could call a shareholders' meeting for the purpose of reorganizing management. All the shareholders, including the minority shareholders who had brought misery to the bank, attended. The atmosphere was uncomfortable for these minority shareholders because they knew that their past practices had been fully exposed. Karmaka was very straightforward about revealing all the facts. He no longer hesitated to point fingers directly at the wrongdoers. One by one, he presented the audit team's findings, revealing all the illegal and unethical practices. He told the gathered shareholders about the improper loan practices. He laid out how these individuals had sold confiscated property at low prices and used bank funds improperly. The managers responsible admitted to all these wrongdoings.

Karmaka no longer had feelings of reluctance, hesitation, or fear. The participants made no comments. The accused minority holders had been cornered.

After presenting the evidence of the dishonest managers' improper conduct, Karmaka arrived at the essence of what he desired, which was to change the management structure. "As a result, I request that all directors and supervisors resign from their positions," he announced.

Then, Karmaka put forward a second proposal. He said, "The number of directors should not be too large. For efficiency and better control, at this moment, two directors should be sufficient. I myself will be the president director of the bank."

All those attending were shocked, especially the guilty individuals, but there was little they could do. Though the dishonest minority shareholders did not find this proposal acceptable, they had been cornered that day and they knew that the change was inevitable. Karmaka was representing the majority shareholder, his father-in-law. Karmaka did not want to waste any more time. He immediately called for a vote. "Of course we won the vote," he recalls.

Therefore, Karmaka legally became the president director of Bank NISP.

After the decision was made, the former management silently left, even before the meeting came to a close. They were very angry as they left the room, but it was the anger of defeat.

Karmaka paid no attention to their anger. He was determined to be the best bank leader he could be. The memory of these individuals ridiculing him a few months back was still fresh in his mind.

At that time, the leader of the bank said something to the other directors in Dutch. Since Dutch was used only by the educated elite and not understood by common people, the leader clearly thought that Karmaka would not understand, but Karmaka knew a little Dutch.

The leader called him shameless for wanting to lead the bank without a college degree. "It was very humiliating," says Karmaka.

But later, those words become very useful to Karmaka. Although the speaker had meant the words to belittle him, Karmaka used them to goad himself into proving to himself that he could do the job.

Karmaka's determination led to victory. In less than a year, NISP fully recovered. Customers' anger subsided. The bank reimbursed the three thousand customers for their "purchase" of the Impalas using the proceeds of the confiscated properties, including the confiscated 43 percent of Bank NISP shares.

Karmaka was very grateful to all the staff and workers. "They were the ones who made the recovery and smooth running of the bank possible," Karmaka reminisces.

However, some of the staff misunderstood the praise that Karmaka gave. One employee surprised Karmaka when he claimed that he was representing the core staff of NISP in saying that it was only proper that some of the bank shares be awarded to them. "We are asking for 20 percent of the shares," said the representative. "Otherwise, we are all going to quit the bank, and the bank will again be disrupted," he threatened.

Upon hearing the threat, Karmaka was truly shocked. He tried to remain calm. On the one hand, Karmaka had to admit that the person was smart and hardworking. However, he had no right to own bank shares. Anyway, if he gave those shares away, his father-in-law would no longer be the controlling shareholder.

Karmaka tried to cool himself. He did not want to respond to the request right away. He simply told the employee representative that he would need his father-in-law's permission. He explained that, because Lim Khe-Tjie was abroad, responding to the request would take two to three months. He needed to buy time. He needed to find a way to keep the bank intact by not giving away family shares. The two to three months should be enough to come up with a strategy.

Meanwhile, Karmaka began to come down to the bank floor and communicate directly with his staff. He especially wanted to get to know the second-tier staff—those who worked directly below the department heads. Karmaka would tell these employees to work hard and be willing to learn from the heads of their department. He thought that if the second-level staff could master their supervisors' jobs, then even if the rebellious core staff really did quit, NISP could still operate without disruption.

More importantly, Karmaka wanted to know why some of the staff were threatening him. He investigated and found out that the heads of department represented by the person who had come requesting the shares had family ties among themselves. He understood why they were able to act in concert. He knew that giving in to such tactics might embolden others to bring up more or different kinds of threats in the future.

Therefore, Karmaka was determined to upgrade the skills of the second-level staff. "If you are willing to work hard and are able to fulfill the requirements, you could become a manager," he told the employees, encouraging them to learn their jobs better.

When Karmaka felt he was ready with the newly trained personnel, he called back in the disloyal manager. "Listen, I have talked to my father-in-law. He can't agree to your request," Karmaka told the representative.

Karmaka then gave the manager a "lecture," saying that people who worked did not always have to stay in one place. "Especially smart people like you; you'd be accepted in many other places. You'd probably have a better chance of developing your career someplace else," Karmaka told him. "Therefore, if you would like to quit, I have no objection. Maybe it would even be better if you quit right now, so that you all would have time to prepare for the next job."

The manager still tried to threaten Karmaka. "Are you sure about that decision?" he countered. "Won't you regret it later?"

Karmaka simply replied by thanking him for his services while at NISP.

In a rage, the representative left Karmaka's office, declaring he would quit NISP.

This manager quit, along with two others. "*Two!*" Karmaka recalls.

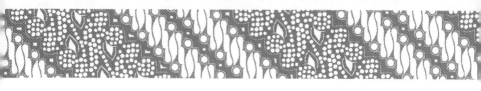

CHAPTER SIXTEEN

ANOTHER DAY, ANOTHER STORM

Bank NISP had twice weathered storms that had almost sunk it, and now clear sailing seemed to lie ahead. But Karmaka was no weatherman, and he could not know that the calm after gaining control of the bank was deceptive. Another storm loomed over the horizon.

This new storm began with the auction of the 43 percent of shares belonging to the fraudulent managers, shares that the High Court had confiscated in order to repay customers who'd ordered the Impalas. On the one hand, the auction was good news because the bank's customers could get their money back and the bank's name would no longer be dragged through the mud. Furthermore, Karmaka would not have to have further dealings with those shareholders who had driven the bank almost to bankruptcy.

On the other hand, Karmaka had no control over who the buyer of the shares would be. He was very curious to see who would emerge as the new shareholders. Perhaps he had leaped out of the frying pan only to find himself in the fire or, as the Indonesian phrase goes, had "gotten out of the crocodile's pond into the lion's den." He had managed to defeat the crocodile, but what if the lion was a very hungry one, waiting to devour him?

However, Karmaka was optimistic and hoped that the buyer would be a good partner, who would help Bank NISP grow.

While Karmaka was contemplating all kinds of possibilities, he received an unexpected visitor—a big, burly man with an apparent air of authority. But something seemed inauthentic about the man. The guest seemed to think that authority could be faked or created out of thin air. In reality, authority is a reflection of an internal strength of character.

Karmaka mentally prepared himself for a battle. *What could this person want?* he asked himself. His instinct told him that the man was up to no good.

Karmaka's intuition proved correct. The man represented the buyer of the 43 percent of shares. He said wanted NISP to sell the remaining 57 percent to him—to give him 100 percent control of NISP. That kind of offer was common in business. What was uncommon was that the person presenting the offer was arrogant and threatening. "You must sell your shares to us within three days. Otherwise, you will know who we are," the representative said.

Karmaka, who had already been tested and hardened in life, handled this new challenge with calm. He tried to be patient, sympathetic, and humble, but at the same time he wanted to signal that they must discuss the request amicably. Karmaka tried to politely indicate that the transaction would not be as the representative had imagined.

The representative, hearing Karmaka's courteous words, did not sense the steel underneath. In fact, Karmaka was determined not to surrender. The representative continued to intimidate. "You must execute the sale immediately," he declared, "for your safety and the safety of your family.

"Don't do anything you'll regret later!" the would-be negotiator said, his pitch rising.

Karmaka kept his cool. Inwardly, he wondered why the calm had not lasted long, why this enormous problem had been thrown at him.

But he had confidence that he could solve this problem as well, so he kept his composure, as well as his resolve. "Sir, maybe we can meet again in a better environment to continue this discussion," Karmaka replied. "Congratulations on winning the auction. Since you are the new bank shareholder, why don't we try partnering for a period of time? Who knows, maybe we were destined by God to work together. It may or may not work out, but we haven't even gotten to know each other yet."

The arrogant representative reacted with sudden and extreme anger. His rage seemed irrational; Karmaka realized though, that by definition, anyone "in a rage" would probably be irrational. "No more talking! You've only got three days," the burly man snarled, while getting up to leave.

Seeing the direction where the new partnership was going, Karmaka got ready to play tough. The self-confidence in his young blood heightened; he told himself that it was time to abandon his polite attitude. Karmaka stood up. In a strong, firm voice, he said "Very well! No need to wait three days. I can answer you right now. We *cannot* fulfill your request!"

The hostile representative appeared to be taking advantage of the fact that Karmaka was an ethnic Chinese minority, a group that was generally perceived to be easily intimidated. Understanding that, Karmaka was forced to try a "weapon" that he wasn't sure would be effective. He had never used this "weapon," but since he was cornered, he decided to give it a try anyway. "My father-in-law owns this bank, and his daughter, my wife, is inheriting it. My father-in-law wants her to develop the business, not to sell it. And my father-in-law is not just any common person," he declared.

The representative appeared puzzled by the phrase "not just any common person." So Karmaka explained further, using the explanation as a means of counter-threatening his opponent. "My father-in-law was a hero of West Java, a freedom fighter for Indonesian Independence," said Karmaka, preparing himself to say what kind of fighter his father-in-law was if he were questioned.

Hearing Karmaka's last words, the representative's attitude changed a bit. Clearly, he did not have the power to make decisions. Finally, he left with his entourage of personal guards, still saying, "You have three days' time. Think it over."

As soon as the visitor left, Karmaka contemplated how to solve this new problem. His safety, as well as the safety of his family, had been threatened. And he had to save the bank.

Finally, Karmaka decided to face the problem head on. He concluded that a representative was usually more aggressive than the boss who sent him. If this proved true in the case at hand, Karmaka guessed optimistically, the owner of the 43 percent shares might, in fact, be a good person; or at least Karmaka might safely conclude that the representative had overacted or that the big man might have misunderstood his boss's real intention. Therefore, Karmaka was determined to meet the boss himself.

On the way to Jakarta to meet the big boss, Karmaka prepared himself for any possibility. If the boss played it soft, he too would play softball. If the boss played it hard, he would play hardball. He was ready to face pressure even worse than that from the representative the day before.

After making inquiries, Karmaka learned that the auction winner was not an ordinary businessman—he was the owner of a very large bank in Jakarta. Karmaka was not acquainted with the new shareholder because NISP was not in the same league as his bank. Karmaka was from the region of Bandung, while the big boss was from Jakarta, Indonesia's capital city. Furthermore, Karmaka managed only a small bank, while the big boss's bank was large and aggressively expanding.

Karmaka was pleasantly surprised when the big boss appeared to be a very nice person; he was willing to see Karmaka, and he was very different from the person he'd sent as his representative. It appeared that Karmaka's preparations for confronting difficult circumstances may have been unnecessary, as the large bank's owner seemed a polite and modest person.

Of course, Karmaka immediately took on a humble attitude. He showed respect to the bigger bank's owner in the most appropriate ways. He offered many thanks that the owner had received him. Karmaka noticed that as he explained why he had come, the big boss observed Karmaka from head to toe. Karmaka could not understand what it meant to be scrutinized in that manner. He guessed that the big boss was reading his personality. Karmaka stayed calm. Finally, the big boss seemed to conclude that Karmaka had the potential to be an ally rather than an antagonist.

The big boss called his assistant in. "This person came from Bandung to discuss the issue of the bank in Bandung," he told his assistant, speaking in the Hokkian Chinese dialect—Karmaka's mother's dialect. "I am busy. You take care of it. Do not bring up my name," the big boss concluded.

The assistant led Karmaka to one of the reception rooms. Karmaka attempted to break the ice, saying "So, you're the winner of the 43 percent of shares of the Bandung bank, right?"

The assistant, acting deaf to Karmaka's opening question, countered with a threat. "So, you're the one who's refusing to sell your shares to us, right?"

Hearing those words Karmaka was simultaneously ready to explode with anger and amused by the cunning of the big boss. However, Karmaka acted as if nothing had happened. He did not intend to smile or frown. From the assistant's attitude Karmaka sensed that the situation was not as good as he had thought when he'd met the big boss. He immediately understood that the boss and the assistant were in fact playing "good cop/bad cop." Karmaka concluded that their original mission of owning 100 percent of NISP shares was still in force. Such behavior was normal from a big bank.

However, Karmaka had no intention of selling his bank. It had a long history and it was a legacy of his father-in-law's family. So there was no meeting ground, and no compromise could be made.

"Just to let you know, in three days, the transaction has to be completed; otherwise, it will be too late," said the assistant.

With this additional repeated threat, Karmaka set up his own battleground. He immediately abandoned his polite façade and stood up from his seat. He frowned. "Hey! I didn't come here to beg," he shouted loudly. "I am not a beggar!" He was very angry and offended by the assistant's threats. He launched his counterthreat. "I came here only to tell you all that if you dare to do anything to us in Bandung, you will be buried alive in Bandung," he declared menacingly.

When the assistant did not interrupt him, Karmaka continued his threat. "You people should know that I only need to tell the freedom fighters over there what you've been up to, and all of you will be finished," he snarled. "You should know that the founder of Bank NISP, my father-in-law, is well known and well respected in Bandung. He was one of its most honored freedom fighters. If you dare go to Bandung, it will be the end of all of you."

After that, Karmaka walked straight out of the room, went out to his car, opened his car door, and got ready to drive back to Bandung.

Surprisingly, the assistant came running out to Karmaka and grabbed his shirt. "Let's talk again," he said. "This must be a misunderstanding."

Eventually, the larger bank accepted Karmaka's proposal to try working together as partners in Bank NISP. But to obtain a formal final agreement, Karmaka had to wait to see the person with authority.

Karmaka started to feel a bit relieved. His firmness in counterthreatening the other side seemed to have worked. The fact that his opponent believed his threats amused him. "Actually, I did not know the details of my father-in-law's heroism during the Revolution," Karmaka remembers with a laugh. Karmaka was tough, but he could also be humorous; in fact, he laughed a lot.

After waiting about half an hour, finally Karmaka met the person with authority. They went to the big boss's room. Before permitting him to enter, guards searched Karmaka for weapons. His talk of revolutionary freedom fighters must have created a suspicion that Karmaka might have obtained permission to carry a gun.[7]

"Yes, my assistant has explained things to me; it was, in fact, a misunderstanding," the person with authority said. "I agree. Let us work together. I will be the chairman of the board of supervisors, and you will be the president of the board of directors."

Karmaka felt a great relief. His heart was at peace. He had resolved another crisis.

---

[7]   In Indonesia, it is a crime to carry a gun without a permit.

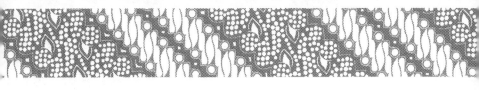

CHAPTER SEVENTEEN

TWO MURDER ATTEMPTS

With pride and delight, Karmaka reported to his father-in-law, who was still in Hong Kong and unable to return to Indonesia, on how he had been able to solve the difficulties with the new owner of 43 percent of the bank's shares. Lim Khe-Tjie was proud that, once again, his son-in-law had succeeded in solving a problem that NISP faced. Even in those days, when telephone communication was not as convenient as it is today, Karmaka always tried to report on the bank's progress to his father-in-law. "'Once in a while I asked for his opinion," says Karmaka. From the other side, Lim Khe-Tjie would call on occasion to discuss issues concerning NISP's well-being.

However, it seemed that Karmaka was not destined to enjoy any period of peacefulness for too long. One day, after *Idhul Fithri*, the Islamic New Year celebration, Karmaka was planning to go out of town. Before leaving, his driver noticed a bullet hole in the left bumper of the car. "Yesterday I did not see this hole. I clean this part of the car every day," the diver reported to Karmaka. Could it be that a stray bullet hit his car?

Karmaka was immediately suspicious. Maybe a malicious person had intentionally shot at his car, using the New Year's festivities, a time when firecrackers were regularly lit, to mask the sound of the gunshot. Karmaka asked the police to investigate.

Their conclusion confirmed Karmaka's suspicions; the bullet had not ricocheted from elsewhere but had been aimed at the car from a short distance, at about a 45-degree angle from the left rear side.[8] "Then the police warned Karmaka to be careful and stay alert. "Someone attempted to kill you," the officer told him.

This incident reminded Karmaka of something that had happened not long after he had fired one of NISP's managers. "At that time, someone also tried to kill me. That made two murder attempts," says Karmaka.

Several months before Karmaka's driver discovered the bullet hole in the car—at a time when Karmaka had never imagined that anyone would try to kill him—Karmaka had just taken over the bank's president director position. The former manager was supposed to hand over the official car. But the former executive did not hand it over right away, saying that the car was under repair. This seemed strange because there was nothing wrong with the car. When Karmaka finally received the car, he became suspicious of the repair job and immediately asked his driver to examine the car.

During his inspection, the driver found something very disturbing that could have been fatal to Karmaka: When the driver stepped on the brake, there was *no* resistance at all! "*Rem ngajeblong*," the driver told him, "empty brake" in the Sunda dialect. "I was lucky that the car had not been used to go out of town. If it had, on a downhill slope, just imagine what could have happened to me!" Karmaka says. Karmaka immediately confronted the former user of the car, angrily taking the former executive to task for having first ruined the bank and then attempting to take his life.

"It's clear that you are plotting to kill me," Karmaka declared. "You aren't satisfied with leading NISP to ruin. You and your colleagues brought NISP to the brink of bankruptcy."

---

8   Drivers drive on the right side of the road in Indonesia.

The former manager denied the accusation, but Karmaka countered with facts and a witness, his driver.

"I'll put it to you simply. If something happens to me in the future, you will be the prime suspect," Karmaka told the former manager. With that, Karmaka left right away. The most important thing was to let the fired executive know that his evil scheme had been uncovered and to leave him with a stern warning.

CHAPTER EIGHTEEN

CAPTIVE IN THE RICE FIELDS

The two attempts to take Karmaka's life only made him mentally stronger. The experience of facing and then successfully escaping from danger made him mentally and spiritually as strong as steel. Karmaka knew he would need to stay alert but not give into fear and become a coward. Karmaka would not run scared; every day, he would conduct his life as he normally would, including carrying his baby out of the house into the front yard in the mornings.

One morning, Karmaka was carrying his baby girl, Parwati, who was then ten months old, the same age he had been when his mother carried him away from the family's village home in Hokjia, China, for the journey across the South China Seas to Indonesia. Parwati was the family's second daughter. She would later (in the 1990s) become the bank director and play an important role in modernizing NISP and much later would become CEO of the bank.

While Karmaka was pleasantly rocking baby Parwati in his arms, he heard a jolting screech! A large vehicle came to a sudden stop in front of him. Karmaka recognized the vehicle as a *GAZ*, a Russian-made military vehicle similar to a jeep. A few men in military uniforms got out of the vehicle and approached Karmaka. One of them glared at him and then said, "Do you know Mr. Tan's house?"

"No, I don't," Karmaka answered. "I don't know any Mr. Tan around here." Without a word, the military men got back onto the *GAZ* and left just like that. However, about thirty minutes later, the telephone rang in the house. Karmaka himself happened to pick up the phone. "Can I talk to the person who was carrying a baby in front of this house?" the voice asked loudly.

"Yes, that was I," answered Karmaka.

The caller said brusquely: "Come immediately to the front of Sin-A Restaurant. Don't tell anyone, even your wife," said the caller. Sin-A Restaurant, on Suniaraja Road, would later house Jasa Arta Bank. "If you don't get there within an hour, grenades will explode around your house," the caller threatened.

Karmaka tried to ask who the caller was, but he got no answer, and the caller hung up. Karmaka was taken aback and uncertain as to what to do. Karmaka's first thought was to avoid harm to his wife and children. What if the grenades really exploded? Then his wife and children would be their victims. With that thought and without telling his wife, he took a rickshaw tricycle to the location the caller had indicated.

Once Karmaka arrived, a man approached him. The man wore a jacket and carried a gun hung on his waist. Karmaka looked at the man's face. It was the same person who, half an hour earlier, had come up to him and asked about the whereabouts of Mr. Tan's house. Before Karmaka could even say a word, the man snapped, "Watch out! This is a pistol with a silencer."

"Get in the Jeep," he ordered sharply but not loudly, so as to avoid being overheard by passersby.

Karmaka was momentarily stunned and unsure what he should do, but he tried to avoid getting into the car at first.

"What's the matter?" asked Karmaka.

"Shut up!" was the answer.

"Where are you taking me, sir?

"Don't ask! If you keep asking, I'll shoot you," the man warned. In the car, Karmaka noticed that the man was accompanied by four other people. The car started up, and Karmaka tried again to ask what the problem was and where he was being taken. He needed to know, he explained, because he hadn't left any message with his wife.

"Don't ask!" the man commanded. "You are a criminal! Tomorrow you'll find out for yourself."

The car made several circles around the city then headed to the northern part of Bandung. From there, they drove north past villages and rice paddies. Far ahead in the middle of the rice fields were a few houses. The GAZ stopped in front of one of these houses. Karmaka was ordered to get out of the car. Once he entered the house, the men closed and locked the door. Karmaka peered out and saw two men guarding the house.

All day long inside the quiet house in the middle of the rice fields, Karmaka tried to guess what was really happening. Who was behind the kidnapping? What were his captors' motives? Karmaka was puzzled—nothing was clear, and he had no clues to work with. Karmaka also pondered how he could let his family know about his predicament and imagined his wife's desperation at his sudden disappearance.

By the time evening approached, nothing had changed. Karmaka was still locked in the house without food or drink. The house was a simple brick building with no luxuries. Part of the wall was glass, though it was not a window.

Even when night came, his captors had still made no communication of any sort. His kidnapper's words still hummed in his ears: "Tomorrow you'll find out for yourself." What would happen tomorrow? Should he surrender? Who could he surrender to? And for what? What if he did not surrender? Would he be killed? "Tomorrow, you'll find out for yourself."

Karmaka tried again to communicate with the two guards but failed. He tried to ask permission to go to a toilet, saying that he had a stomachache. The guards flatly refused his request. "Don't play games, you! Wait until tomorrow!" one of the kidnappers barked.

Even though he could not figure out what the kidnappers wanted and who they might be, Karmaka guessed that they must be up to some type of extortion, that they would pressure him to give something up. But what? Money? Shares? It must be something.

Karmaka would not succumb to extortion. And he supposed that refusing to pay the ransom would lead to his being killed. The kidnappers would be enraged if Karmaka did not give them what they wanted. Therefore, his only choice was to escape. Since he was not tied up, it might be possible. He did not sleep. He inspected the interior of the house and tried to estimate the strength of its construction, to see if he could break out. Even though Karmaka had not eaten or drank anything since that morning, he still felt strong. His athletic stamina would help. In addition, his experience in the textile factories and constructing sporting equipment when he was a physical education teacher at Nan Hua would aid him in finding the best place to break out of the house.

Run! That was what he determined to do.

At 2:30 in the morning, he peered out and saw the guards asleep and snoring. Karmaka carefully broke open a window and left behind his shirt and long pants, as well as his shoes. The shirt, pants, and shoes would only hinder his agility. Wearing only his undershirt and pants, he pried open the window and jumped out silently.

Away from the house, Karmaka ran and ran. Thrashing through the dark and silent rice fields, he intentionally ran barefooted so as not to create additional noise. Another reason he had ditched his shoes and clothes was to avoid being identified as rich city folk. The villagers, who were generally very poor, would immediately tag anyone wearing a shirt and long pants as a city dweller.

Karmaka kept running along the causeways that bordered the rice paddy ponds. He passed the narrow roads at the edge of the village. There, he saw a farmer walking alone. "What village is this, Elder?" asked Karmaka in Sundanese, the West Java dialect.

"Gegerkalong," answered the farmer. "Where are you going to?" Karmaka told the farmer that he wanted to get to Hegarmanah Road. Hegarmanah number 10, to be exact. The farmer pointed out the direction. Karmaka kept running. At around 4:00 in the morning, Karmaka arrived at number 10 Hegarmanah Road, the house of an army brigadier general. Karmaka ran toward the home of Brigadier General Sutoko. His father-in-law had once told him that if something serious happened, he should get protection from this high-ranking officer. His father-in-law had not told Karmaka who the person was or how he was related to this prominent figure.

Still panting when he arrived at the address, Karmaka immediately knocked hard at the door.

"Who is it?" a voice asked from inside the house.

"It's me, sir, son-in-law of Lim Khe-Tjie," Karmaka answered. "I'm asking for help and protection," he added. "Someone tried to kill me."

"Lim Khe-Tjie of Bank NISP?" asked the voice inside the house.

"Yes, sir," Karmaka answered.

Soon the door opened. Brigadier General Sutoko himself opened the door. He was taken aback by Karmaka's appearance; the man at his doorstep was rumpled, dirty, tired, and barefoot.

"Come in," said *Pak* Sutoko.[9] "Sit here," he added kindly.

Karmaka would later learn that Sutoko was a prominent military figure in the army's Siliwangi division, stationed in West Java, and a key military figure of the Republic of Indonesia. He had been a proponent of establishing Indonesia as a centralized government rather than a federation of states during the Indonesian Revolution for the nation's independence. He was also an important officer trusted by the

---

[9] The word *Pak*, derived from *Bapak* (father) is used as an honorific before a person's name.

powerful General Nasution of the famous Siliwangi division. During the student movement of the 1960s to topple the first Indonesian president, President Sukarno, General Sutoko was known to be close to the students. When some of the student leaders from ITB were in danger of being arrested by the authorities, Sutoko had assured their safety. After retirement, he had gone into business and was active in education. His son, Dr. Mame Slamet Sutoko, was the rector of Widyatama University, an outstanding university in Bandung.

Once Karmaka had taken his seat, General Sutoko asked Karmaka to recount what had happened to him. When Karmaka finished telling him the story from beginning to end, General Sutoko was astonished.

"Do you know who your father-in-law is?" interrupted *Pak* Sutoko.

"Yes, Lim Khe-Tjie," answered Karmaka.

"Not that. Do you know who he really is?" asked *Pak* Sutoko.

"No, I don't know," Karmaka answered.

Pak Sutoko explained that Lim Khe-Tjie was a hero of the Indonesian struggle for independence.

That very morning General Sutoko called a colonel. He explained to the colonel that someone had attempted to murder Karmaka, so he needed protection.

At about 5:00 in the morning, the colonel arrived, accompanied by several of his soldiers. Right away, the soldiers escorted Karmaka to the colonel's house. From there, ten soldiers escorted Karmaka home. Some of these soldiers would keep in touch with Karmaka for years to come, and one of their children would become a loyal employee of NISP.

Karmaka was under continuous personal protection for two years, although he was guarded by only two soldiers, not ten. His guards gave him a bulletproof vest and requested that he wear it whenever he was outdoors. "All of this made me feel uncomfortable. Not only was the jacket heavy, but I was also worried that people would think I was a snob," recalls Karmaka. "But, what could I do? I wanted to be alive to rescue my father-in-law's business."

With Brigadier General Sutoko.

CHAPTER NINETEEN

A PATRIOT IN THE STRUGGLE
FOR INDEPENDENCE

If Karmaka had never been kidnapped, he would not have gone to General Sutoko for protection and would probably never have learned about his father-in-law's role in the struggle for independence. When Lim Khe-Tjie had said, "If anything happens endangering your life, ask for protection from *Pak* Sutoko," Karmaka had not dared to ask who this prominent figure was. He had not known what relationship his father-in-law had with a person of such distinction in the Siliwangi military.

"Your father-in-law was the person whom we entrusted to smuggle weapons into Indonesia through the port of Surabaya City. Then we distributed the weapons to the Revolution's guerilla fighters," Sutoko told him. Sutoko explained that Karmaka was given protection because his father-in-law was a hero of Indonesian independence.

Pak Sutoko described how once the weapons were in Cirebon, Lim Khe-Tjie would immediately send them to his friend, Tan Lin-Tjik, who owned the textile factory NV Padasuka in the town of Majalaya, south of Bandung. Many of the guerilla fighters were housed in that factory. During the day, the soldiers disguised themselves as factory workers; at night, they carried their guns. One of the fighters who pretended to be a worker was, in fact, a high-ranking military officer.

Karmaka was surprised by the explanation. He remembered the threats he'd used against the big boss from the bank in Jakarta, bluffing that his father-in-law was a revolutionary hero. At that time, he had not known for sure whether what he said was true. Indeed, he'd vaguely remembered hearing about his father-in-law's heroism once, but he had not paid attention to the details and had never tried to find out the truth. It was a relief to find out that what he'd said had not been a bluff after all; in fact, he had been telling the truth! He felt even more proud of his father-in-law and his friend, Tan Lin-Tjik, the owner of the NV Padasuka textile factory, where he had worked for five years. Working in that textile factory had taught him how to become a good businessman and leader.

"If the guerilla fighters needed clothing, medicine, food, or money," continued General Sutoko, "they would send a courier to Tan Lin-Tjik, who would then contact your father-in-law to raise money. Your father-in-law, Lim Khe-Tjie, would immediately collect donations from his friends to purchase the supplies."

The general added that Lim Khe-Tjie was also able to obtain important information from the Dutch side about plans to attack guerillas bases. He immediately transmitted such information to Tan Lin-Tjik. The latter would then secretly pass the information on to guerila leaders, including Sutoko. "If there hadn't been such intelligence activities, more of our guerila fighters would have died," Sutoko said.

He explained that the Dutch never suspected Lim Khe-Tjie because his relationship with the guerilla fighters was a secret from almost everyone. There was, deliberately, no apparent relationship between the two parties. Everything went through Tan Lin-Tjik. With this arrangement, Lim Khe-Tjie was free to move in many matters without anyone suspecting which side he was on. He still maintained close relationships with the Dutch intelligence personnel, who were his friends.

While waiting for the colonel who was arranging for Karmaka to be protected from further assassination attempts, Sutoko continued to narrate the story of Lim Khe-Tjie and the Revolution. He told Karmaka that he had given Lim Khe-Tjie a number of tasks. One of the tasks that Sutoko had entrusted Lim Khe-Tjie with required him to be away for long periods of time. No one, not even his own wife, was to know where he was or how long he would be gone. While Lim Khe-Tjie was on that assignment, Sutoko heard that Lim's wife often cried because her husband was away, at times for months, without saying good-bye or sending a message of any kind. His wife thought he had been captured by the guerilla fighters, since everyone knew that he was close to the Dutch officials. To comfort her, one day Sutoko sent one of the guerilla fighters, disguised as a postal carrier from the main postal office at Bandung's Gedung Sate building. The "postman" delivered a letter at Lim Khe-Tjie's house, informing Lim's wife that her husband was all right and would be back in another few days.

Of course Lim's wife did not believe what her visitor said. The "postman" further tried to convince her by saying, "I guarantee his speedy return. Your husband is definitely fine because he is a truly good person."

Much later, the "postman" was revealed to be one of the most exceptional guerilla fighters, a man who, after Indonesia gained independence, became deputy to General Nasution, one of the most famous generals in modern Indonesian history.

Sutoko went on to tell Karmaka that Lim Khe-Tjie was, in fact, one of the seven Chinese from Bandung chosen to receive the very prestigious Freedom Fighters Heroes service medal. But Lim Khe-Tjie did not want to accept the medal. When asked why, he explained. "I am afraid that it will jeopardize my relationship with my Dutch friends, who entrusted me with information about plans to attack guerilla bases," Lim told Sutoko. After independence, these Dutch friends continued to live in Bandung and maintain friendships with Lim Khe-Tjie.

After the detailed account that General Sutoko related, Karmaka not only felt admiration for his father-in-law, but also realized that the story could be important evidence in his efforts to bring Lim Khe-Tjie home to Indonesia from Hong Kong. Given a heroic background of that magnitude, Karmaka could not abide the fact that his father-in-law, whose passport had been invalidated by slander and accusations, was being prevented from returning to Indonesia. It had been six years since Lim Khe-Tjie had been detained in Hong Kong and forced to live there, after what was supposed to be a short trip in 1959 for his whole family to pay homage to their ancestors' graves in Hokjia, China.

Lim Khe-Tjie often expressed his longing to be back in Bandung. "When he contacted me from Hong Kong, my father-in-law always conveyed his homesickness for his homeland, Indonesia," Karmaka remembers.

When he fell seriously ill in Hong Kong, Lim Khe-Tjie made a final wish. He said, "When the time comes for me to die, please take my body to Indonesia and bury me there".

To the Chinese, choosing one's burial place—the place where one comes to permanent rest—is an expression of love for and commitment to that place. For Lim Khe-Tjie, that place was Indonesia.

NISP Bank founder, Karmaka's father-in-law Lim Khe Tjie.

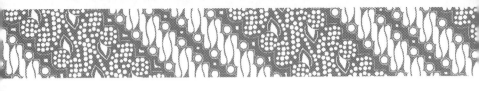

CHAPTER TWENTY

DEFENDING AN EMPLOYEE

Thanks to the protection Brigadier General Sutoko of the Siliwangi Army Division offered, Karmaka was able to perform his duties as president of directors of Bank NISP in relative security, and the bank enjoyed a period of smooth operations. Karmaka eventually became accustomed to wearing the bulletproof vest, and most importantly, NISP was able to operate well and begin to grow normally again, a significant accomplishment in the very difficult economic conditions still prevailing in the country.

But the pleasure of working in peace did not last long. Suddenly, in September 1965, Indonesia plunged into a very chaotic situation both politically and economically, endangering social cohesion and public safety. The government took the drastic action of redenominating the nation's currency to fight inflation, making 1,000 rupiah worth only 1 rupiah! This action immediately caused a great panic, especially among those who saved their money in a bank. All savings banks, including NISP, were invaded by customers whose savings had suddenly shrunk one thousand times in value. The customers were in an uncontrollable rage. They could no longer differentiate between those who should be blamed and those who were blameless. They were understandably angry because the money they had earned during their lifetime had suddenly and dramatically lost its value, becoming close to worthless. Karmaka and his staff tried to explain to the customers that the bank could not be blamed. But the customers were in no mood to understand. Many bank staff members were assaulted by enraged customers who demanded the return of their money as recorded in their saving books and refused to accept the new denomination. Heads of department were beaten, spit upon, locked up, and even kidnapped.

One time, Karmaka was told that there was a very angry military colonel who was about to beat a bank officer. Karmaka came downstairs and saw the colonel grabbing the banker's neck. Karmaka rushed in and pulled the colonel's arm away from the man. "He is my employee! Don't hit him!" shouted Karmaka.

But the colonel was uncontrollable and hit Karmaka hard in his jaw. Karmaka's mouth was filled with blood, and he lost one of his teeth.

The colonel, still in a frenzy, shouted that he had been sent into lethal battles and had survived; he wanted to know why he was not safe putting his money in NISP? His life savings and retirement fund had disappeared; one million rupiah in savings had suddenly become only one thousand rupiah.

Karmaka and the bank staff explained again and again to the outraged colonel that the government, not the bank, had made the decision to devalue the rupiah, but the colonel refused to accept their explanations.

Bank employees had more than just angry customers to deal with. Political instability created an environment in which local authorities apprehended some staff members, charging them with the crime of belonging to an underground movement associated with the communist political party.

As a result of such terrible situations, all NISP offices were essentially paralyzed. At that time, NISP had fifty-six branches with

3,362 employees. Since the employees could not safely perform their jobs, none of the branches dared to open.

"I was terrified, confused, frustrated, hopeless, and sad, all mixed together," says Karmaka. "I screamed and screamed like a madman. The bank that I had guarded with my life and my many sacrifices and much suffering had come to that."

Karmaka was very concerned for the safety of his managers and bank officers, who had been very loyal and hardworking. They were also public figures in the communities in each of their regions. More than that, they had suffered for the bank, and Karmaka had promised them that, once Bank NISP was doing well, their welfare would be improved. "They had suffered, they had worked hard for so long, and the rewards they had been waiting for should not have been very long in arriving. But then, suddenly, the hope and the anticipation evaporated just like that," Karmaka remembers.

He could not accept such a situation. He could not grasp why such a thing had happened. He had not done anything wrong; neither had the managers or leaders of the branches or of any of the bank employees. Why had they become victims, with no rescue in sight?

Of the fifty-six NISP offices, only two could still open—the headquarters in Bandung and the main branch office in Jakarta. Branches that had been running well and growing, like those in Medan, Palembang, Padang, Lampung, Manado, Banjarmasin, Surabaya, Semarang, Denpasar, and other cities had to be closed. In addition, the political situation had escalated into a massive crisis created by a failed coup d'état. Indeed, the years from 1966 to 1968 were among the most chaotic and bloodiest ever in modern Indonesian history.

In the middle of the financial crisis caused by bank runs and customers converting their national currency into US dollars, the Central Bank ordered recapitalization of all national banks. NISP, which was licensed only as a savings bank, suffered bank runs since it could not convert customers' rupiah deposits into foreign currency. The Central Bank ordered NISP's shareholders to inject new capital in the amount of six million rupiah, an amount that technically put NISP in great danger of bankruptcy. The Central Bank would not allow banks with insufficient capital to exist, in spite of the fact that shortage of capital was the consequence of the government's own regulations. The Central Bank ordered bank shareholders to solve the problem by injecting more capital of their own. If a bank should fail, it would be taken over or liquidated. The Central Bank allotted each bank only six month's time in which to increase capital.

Karmaka immediately communicated with his bank partner, the big boss in Jakarta who had won the auction for 43 percent of NISP bank shares. In accordance with the regulations, the big boss would have to proportionally inject 43 percent of the six million rupiah needed, while Karmaka's wife, who owned 57 percent, would likewise inject her proportion of the capital.

The Jakarta banker refused to put up the money, claiming that he was not capable due to the current economic situation. Instead, he asked Karmaka to take over his shares, but he did not want to sell them at a loss. Rather, he offered the shares at twice the value than what they had held at the time he bought them. Of course, Karmaka flatly refused the offer. "NISP's capital shortage was not due to the faults of management, but the consequence of government regulations," says Karmaka.

The tough negotiations went on with both parties being stubborn and under great tension. Understandably, the big boss did not want to lose out. Moreover, like Karmaka, he himself was in deep troubles with his own bank.

Finding it difficult to get Karmaka to yield, the big boss finally asked only for compensation. He asked for NISP's prime office building on Gunung Sahari Road; in return, he would transfer the 43 percent shares to Karmaka's wife. Karmaka rejected this proposal outright, as 43 percent of NISP shares were worthless compared to real estate such as the NISP office building. With such an exchange, Karmaka's wife would certainly be the loser.

Once the big boss realized that Karmaka would reject any proposal that was only advantageous to his bank, he came to his final conclusion. "Let's close the bank and have it liquidated," he said.

To Karmaka, closing the bank would be like killing his own baby—a baby that had gone through serious illness for a long time but had recovered, thanks to Karmaka's dedication and struggles, and had been growing up to be become an energetic young lad.

Realistically, Karmaka understood that the big boss's Jakarta bank was facing the same unpleasant fate as was NISP. In fact, that bank was much larger and faced even greater problems than those of NISP. Karmaka came to the realization that he could not deny this fact. This time, he did not want to quarrel with the big boss and create further animosity between them. But if he bought the big boss's shares, Karmaka was trapped between two high-risk obligations—preserving NISP from liquidation and carrying the total burden of fulfilling 100 percent of the capital injection required by regulation.

In the middle of the quandary, Karmaka had to make a choice. In spite of the big unknowns, he chose to preserve NISP. "I would rather die than to sentence my father-in-law's bank to its death and sacrifice all its innocent employees along with it," he determined.

Having made this decision, Karmaka now turned to the hard work of finding people willing to buy the 43 percent of shares at the price the big boss had set. It was very difficult to find buyers, as buying worthless shares did not make sense. The only selling point that he could offer to potential buyers was that the owner of the bank was the family of Lim Khe-Tjie, whose reputation had never been doubted. Karmaka also offered a promise that he himself would run the management of the bank and would work as hard he could to increase the value of the shares.

In such a chaotic situation, it was almost impossible to find investors. Moreover, even if he were to procure enough buyers, he would still have many difficulties to overcome. For example, he would have to rebuild the bank branches; appease the still angry customers; solve the problems of compensating more than three thousand employees who had lost their jobs, and, above all, solve his own problem of citizenship. His application to become a naturalized Indonesian citizen, which only the president could approve, was still pending. Yet, without Indonesian citizenship, he could not hold the directorship of the bank. The three-year special permit allowing him to direct the bank would expire within a year and could not be extended.

To prevent Bank Indonesia from closing NISP, Karmaka had no choice but to take on the significant risk of borrowing the required 6 billion rupiah (old currency) capital injection. This courageous sacrifice would put a very heavy mental burden on him. He knew that failure would lead him to commit suicide and his innocent family would be sacrificed. But this was the road Karmaka felt compelled to follow.

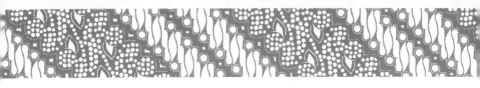

CHAPTER TWENTY-ONE

ENDLESS PROBLEMS
WITHOUT SOLUTIONS

Karmaka had contacted several potential buyers for the 43 percent of shares that had belonged to the banker from Jakarta. However, none of them was interested in becoming a partial owner of Bank NISP, given its troubled situation. Nevertheless, Karmaka did not give up. He remembered that NISP was a member of Perbanas (National Association of Private Banks), and he wondered if the association could help. The chairman of Perbanas was also commissioner of a major private bank. Karmaka approached him and asked if his bank would be interested in purchasing the shares.

Fortunately, his efforts were not in vain. NISP engaged in negotiations with the major private bank, and the two banks completed the deal. Karmaka now had a new partner. Having a new partner did not mean that NISP could solve the problems it faced, but at the very least, NISP would avoid being closed down. As such, Karmaka felt more at ease. He could start focusing on how to revive NISP, where to start, and what NISP's future might be.

Karmaka realized that being a savings bank was not the right model. He had learned from his experiences during the economic crisis, when the national currency was devalued, that many middle—to low-income customers had suffered. Karmaka saw with his own eyes the impact of currency devaluation on small account holders, such as civil servants, soldiers, and retirees. It was true that he himself was also the victim of devaluation, but the majority of bank depositors suffered proportionally more. He did not have the heart to see his customers devastated again if another economic crisis should befall.

It dawned on Karmaka that he should change the focus of the bank from a savings bank to a much more diversified commercial bank. Of course, such a change would not be an easy thing to do, as the bank would have many more new requirements to fulfill. But Karmaka was determined to do so because the survival of NISP depended on it. To him, this plan would be written in stone.

In the reigning environment of severe political turmoil, economic meltdowns, and tighter commercial bank requirements, Bank NISP would have to be condensed. The commercial bank planned could not afford, in the beginning, to operate with many branches. It would have to start with only two offices—one in Bandung that would function as the bank's headquarters and the other a branch office in the capital, Jakarta. What would happen to the rest of the branches? They would have to be closed.

Already, the political and economic turmoil had forced the closing of the branches one by one. The fate of the more than 3,200 employees and sales agents was Karmaka's biggest concern. He did not have the heart to let these employees go. He remembered their dedication during crisis after crisis. He remembered their loyalty. He remembered their hard work and sacrifices, even though they could not be compensated as they deserved. But Karmaka's rational brain told him that to ensure the bank's survival, only two branches could exist. The remaining fifty branches had to be closed, and a massive lay off would be the result.

For the two branches, Karmaka would need only 100 employees—60 in Bandung and 40 in Jakarta. The rest—3,262 employees—would have to be laid off. Karmaka did not know how to communicate the bad news to them. Would the employees understand? What should he say to them? He remembered that the relationship between the employees and the bank was like that of a big family.

With sadness, Karmaka was forced to come up with severance pay money. Calculations showed that the bank's funds were not sufficient to cover the severance payments. He would have to take on personal loans. NISP offered the employees ten months' salary as severance. "The difficulty was how to make the employees understand," he recalls.

The employees rejected the proposal of severance pay, and the situation became heated. The employees launched protests; they posted all kinds of placards condemning Karmaka, labeling him a cruel person.

On top of this, Karmaka discovered a complication with NISP's new partner. The new big bank partner was continuously short on cash liquidity. As a result, the owner kept borrowing NISP's money to make up for the shortfall, while NISP itself was in need of capital. Disastrously, the new partner drained nearly 40 billion rupiah of NISP's funds.

Karmaka expressed his concerns to the partner. The reply was troubling. "What's the use of owning NISP if I cannot take advantage of it to help my troubled bank?" he said.

Karmaka was at a loss as to what to do. Finally, he had no choice but to run helter-skelter among close contacts of his father-in-law in search of loans. As these were private loans, Karmaka would be personally responsible for paying the interest. The debt was growing bigger day by day, and soon, he would not be able to pay the interest.

The combination of assaults from the employees, harassment from the lenders, and mounting debts became unsolvable problems Karmaka had to face daily. On the one hand, he wished he could escape from these problems, but on the other hand, he had the burden of responsibilities to his father-in-law and his family.

Facing the debt collectors, he could get away by promising payments with higher interest. However, he could not ignore the turbulence of the employees. Karmaka often met with the employees to try to explain the situation to them rationally. "It is true that I acted cruelly, but it is better for all of you to be laid off with ten months' salary than to let the bank collapse with no severance pay at all for any of you," Karmaka explained. It was true that laying off employees was a bad choice, but it was the lesser evil among the alternatives, one of which was to let the bank collapse.

Of course the employees were not easily convinced. The painting of graffiti continued, including accusations on the walls of NISP buildings. They all accused Karmaka of being a cruel employer.

The employee problem remained unresolved, debt collectors kept calling, and the new partner kept bleeding the bank. Meanwhile, the deadline to present additional capital was fast approaching. If Karmaka could not meet this deadline, the Central Bank would immediately close NISP. The problems seemed to be coming at Karmaka from all sides at the same time, each demanding he resolve it first.

But Karmaka was determined. He decided to overcome the problems without the help of his partner. He decided to make a huge gamble. Karmaka borrowed 6 billion rupiah from seven parties at an interest rate of 15 percent per month, almost 200 percent per year! Karmaka wrote and submitted checks to lenders with a cash date a few months to a year in the future. However, he had to pay the interest in advance. Karmaka simply didn't think about how he would pay off those checks.

This desperate, insane action was the only way to meet the Central Bank's deadline, and doing so was the primary element needed to ensure NISP's survival. Karmaka was like a madman banging his head on the wall. Actually, his head was pounding all the time, as he thought about how he might get the money to pay off the checks.

The clock was ticking. It felt to Karmaka like it was ticking faster and faster. The nation's economy was still in chaos. The nation's politics grew increasingly tense. The NISP employees continued to assault him. The payment date for his checks crept closer and closer.

At such a difficult time, the employees pressed Karmaka for a meeting. They yelled and shouted and demanded their rights. They also refused to be laid off. Karmaka, already stressed, could not take it anymore. He faced the angry employees and screamed like a madman. "Hey, friends, if you do not want accept what I've offered you, just take over the bank! Just take over the management!" he shouted.

"Just take over the bank assets," Karmaka screamed. "But you will have to pay all the bank debts that I personally borrowed from the outside to fulfill Bank Indonesia's 6 million Rupiah requirement!"

After this outburst, Karmaka turned silent; then he wept. His emotions had drained him. He could no longer talk. Karmaka had already given himself up to whatever would happen next.

The employees became quiet. There was no indication of what they were thinking. In his heart, Karmaka knew that his outburst was only because he could no longer hold off the pressure. Even if the employees were to take over the bank, their efforts would be in vain. If they sold all the assets of the bank, it would not even be enough to pay back the bank's debts. Eventually, the employees would get nothing.

After a long silence, the employees started whispering among themselves. A couple of them approached Karmaka. They asked him to be patient. Karmaka would always remember two female employees who approached him; crouched in front of him, they grabbed his feet crying loudly. They told him that they loved NISP and hoped to remain its employees.

The encounter, however, did not mean that they accepted Karmaka's proposal. The problems were still far from resolved. Meanwhile, the first checks were almost due. Karmaka still did not know where he could get the money to pay them off. Karmaka's mind was also haunted by the vision of the 3,262 employees to be laid off and the image of the two female employees grabbing his feet, crying, and pleading to remain with the bank.

Every night found Karmaka sleepless. He would remember his responsibilities to his father-in-law and the family. In the midst of such bewilderment, Karmaka was no longer able to think clearly. His brain was confused; it felt as if a circuit gone haywire had shorted out his brain cells. Karmaka felt that his honor was at stake.

First, he felt ashamed about having to lay off 3,262 employees, the very human spirit of NISP with whom he had been so close. Second, he felt that he had disappointed his father-in-law, even though events were beyond his ability to control them.

He grabbed a piece of paper and wrote some final words to be left behind. When he had written all the parting messages, he reached for a bottle of poison. Karmaka drank it. He had chosen to end his life with honor, as if he were a samurai warrior paying for his failures with the honor of death.

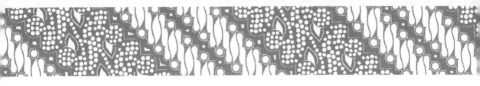

CHAPTER TWENTY-TWO

PLEADING FOR SECRECY

Karmaka was unconscious and in critical condition in his room at home when his wife found him. Karmaka did not know what had happened until he awoke and found himself lying on a bed in Boromeus Hospital in Bandung. Immediately, he knew that his suicide attempt had failed. He felt ashamed and realized what he needed to do.

When the doctor entered his room, Karmaka asked to speak with him. He wanted the doctor to keep what had happened secret. The only other person who knew was his wife. But before Karmaka could ask him, the doctor slapped his face and yelled, "Why did you do that?" Karmaka felt deeply embarrassed.

After apologizing to the doctor, Karmaka listed the reasons for his suicide attempt, all of which needed to be kept secret. If the public found out, the customers would leave NISP, as would the key staff members, *Pak* Hakim and *Pak* Peter, whom Karmaka considered exceptionally talented. Should they find out about his suicide attempt, they would realize that NISP was at the brink of collapse. Karmaka was worried that they would abandon NISP. If all this were to happen, it would be the end of NISP.

If NISP were to go bankrupt, the victims would be the little people who had put their money into the bank's saving accounts. Low-income wage earners and retirees comprised 90 percent of the bank's customers; the rest were lenders who would at least be compensated if the bank were to be liquidated.

Karmaka explained to the doctor that his suicide attempt was the result of an unbearable mental pressure brought on by a series of unfathomable predicaments—the mounting debts and interest payment due that he could never pay out; the heartbreaking layoffs of 3,200 loyal employees that he could not avoid; the large sum of severance pay that he could not provide; and the responsibilities and honor he owed to his father-in-law, his family, and the community at large.

The doctor, who incidentally was a customer of NISP, listened intently to Karmaka. He felt moved by Karmaka's story and was sympathetic to Karmaka's plight. He agreed to keep the suicide attempt out of public knowledge. He honored Karmaka's request and placed a sign in front of the room, which stated that Karmaka was in an acute condition and could not accept any visitors as precaution against Karmaka being pursued by angry employees.

Karmaka began to regret what he had done. He wondered how he could have committed such an irresponsible act. He also deeply regretted that he had jeopardized the fate of his wife and children, as well as that of NISP and all the good people at the bank who depended on him for their livelihood.

Karmaka felt sad and remorseful. However, his spirit once again rose from the ashes. He chose to continue the fight for NISP's survival, resolving to always listen to his beloved wife, who encouraged him to never give up. He firmly believed that, in order to revive NISP, he needed to upgrade the bank from a savings bank to a commercial bank, starting with two banks only. Sadly, this meant that he still had to find a way to lay off 3,200 employees. Moreover, he had to solve the perplexing problem of rain check payments.

What happened to the letters of his last will? Was it too late to retract the words he'd written? Apparently, they had never been sent out, Karmaka immediately retrieved the envelopes containing the letters and tore them up. His wife and the seven gentlemen to whom he'd addressed the letters would never know what the letters said.

CHAPTER TWENTY-THREE

A TOUCHING DISCUSSION IN THE HOSPITAL

As Karmaka had been absent from the office for a while, the employees of NISP began discussing among themselves his whereabouts. The last time they'd seen him, he'd been extremely angry at them. They wondered if he was really so angry that he no longer wanted to take care of the bank.

Eventually the employees heard that Karmaka had been admitted to a hospital and remained in critical condition. Speculation abounded on what would happen if he did not recover. Would someone else rescue NISP? The employees realized that, if such unfortunate circumstances were to come to pass, NISP would definitely be closed; they would lose their jobs, and the chance that they would get severance pay was uncertain. A few employees started to think that it would be better to take Karmaka's offer of ten months' salary than to risk getting nothing at all.

However, most of the employees still rejected the severance pay offer. Although differences of opinions remained, at least the employees had examined the option of accepting Karmaka's offer. The argument between the different factions of employees dragged on, but slowly the majority opinion turned toward accepting the offer, with one condition—severance pay would be twenty times the monthly salary, instead of ten. With the added stipulation, the staunchest group finally mellowed down. The employees added one more condition—only 3,000 employees would be laid off, and NISP would retain the remaining 362 for the operation of its two branches.

Once the employees had reached this agreement, they started to inquire as to where Karmaka was hospitalized and how they could contact him.

During the third week of Karmaka's stay at the hospital, a delegation of employees, led by the head or the bank's personnel department and accompanied by the leader of the labor union, came to see him.

Though the hospital staff would not allow the delegation to enter the room, especially since there were so many of them and they were broaching such a difficult subject, the employees busted through the door and forced their way in. They were surprised to see Karmaka in the condition he was in. His face was pale, and his body, previously ridiculed by the workers as being "fat," was, by that time, bony.

"Respected and beloved *Pak* Kwee[10]," greeted the leader, carefully beginning his speech, "we come here as representatives of the workers of NISP."

Karmaka listened attentively. In his heart, he was surprised to hear words like "respected" and "beloved." He had not heard those words for a very long time. For months, the workers had been throwing harsh words at him, condemning him as a cruel and inhumane person. Their expressions of anger and resentment had pierced Karmaka's heart while the complicated problems demanding solutions packed his head.

---

[10] Karmaka would not change his name until 1966. NISP's employees knew him as "Kwee," his Chinese last name. At this time, his full name was Kwee Tjie-Hui. He could not change his name to an Indonesian one because his request for Indonesian citizenship, which he had submitted more than ten years previously, still lingering ungranted.

"*Pak* Kwee, we did not realize that your illness was so severe," continued the head of the delegation, as the members of the delegation stood by. "We would like to let you know that we, the workers, realize and understand that the bank is in a very difficult situation. However, we earnestly request that our proposal be accepted." The delegation head laid out the proposal the employees had agreed on, asking for both the reduced number of layoffs in return for the resignation of the rest and the increased severance pay.

Karmaka held firm on his position. If he were to compromise, the bank would likely be unable to survive; the delegation's request simply exceeded the bank's financial capacity. In being firm, however, Karmaka had to convey his rejection of the counteroffer with well-chosen words. First, he wanted to express how grateful he was for the employees' visit and polite words. Second, he wanted to show his appreciation of their acceptance of his proposal and that he respected the requested conditions. Third, he had to keep his emotions stable, since he was still not completely well.

"My brothers and sisters[11], our bank is incapable of meeting your conditions. I have borrowed huge sums of money and I am not sure if I can pay them all back. I borrowed on my own private accounts, with the sole purpose of saving the bank," said Karmaka in his opening statement.

"I understand and empathize with how you all feel. As you know, I was once a worker in a textile factory for twelve years. But with great sorrow and concern, I'm telling you all that the bank is unable to fulfill your wishes. It's not that I do not want to help. I do not have the means to fulfill your request. Even the severance pay of ten times your salary needs to be paid to you in six month installments. It cannot be paid all at once. There isn't enough money for it," said Karmaka.

---

[11]   "Brothers and sisters" is a polite means of address in Indonesia.

"I humbly ask for your understanding and acceptance of my earnest proposal," he concluded.

Upon hearing the rejection, the union leader became very angry. "*Pak* Kwee, do not be that cruel. We workers have dedicated our lives to the bank. Now we are victims of unemployment. That's too much!" he said.

Commotion arose as the leader's statement resonated with the workers.[12] The leader, aware of the escalating emotions, instructed the workers to leave the hospital room, knowing that it was inappropriate to make a commotion in a hospital. They continued the debate hotly outside of the room, so loudly that Karmaka could hear. Eventually, the majority opinion turned to accepting Karmaka's offer with his conditions. The workers knew that the dire state of NISP's finances was not the fault of management.

The delegation returned to Karmaka's room. The leader announced their acceptance and stated that the retained workers swore to God that they would strive with all their efforts for the revival and growth of NISP. In a highly emotionally tone, he also expressed the hope that, once the bank returned to good standing, their laid off friends would gradually be rehired. He added, "Even though we were not born in the same place or at the same time, we will strive together with our best

---

12   The word "workers" was in popular use even in the banking business, as the strength of Communist Party of Indonesia was increasing at that time. In 1966 Sukarno, Indonesia's first president, was toppled and replaced by Suharto, and the Communist Party was disbanded. With the New Order government, the term "workers" was changed to the Indonesian word *karyawan*, "employees," which means "one who creates." The objective of the new government was to change the image of working people from that of a rebellious class to a productive one. It was one of the many words used to promote economic development and to attract foreign investments.

efforts to be always with *Pak* Kwee and NISP through the good times and the bad times."

Karmaka was overwhelmed with tears and finally said "yes" to their requests. Then it was time for Karmaka to name his conditions. He explained that the workers who remained at the bank had to be willing to work with no overtime pay and without pay raises for the next five years; the workers had to work until the completion of the day's jobs, and there would not be any extra benefits, such as living expense support. As a consolation, Karmaka promised that if all employees were willing to work with those conditions, then later, when NISP once again became prosperous, the employee welfare systems would be reinstated and improved.

The employees accepted the outcome of the bargaining at the hospital.

Karmaka was very relieved. He felt that his failed suicide attempt could well have been predestined so that he would be able to revive and move NISP forward, with full support and sympathy from the *karyawan*.

Adding to Karmaka's feeling of relief, other blessings, which speeded up his recovery, were to come. He was discharged from the hospital sooner than expected. Karmaka was very moved by *Pak* Peter and *Pak* Hakim, the two most loyal and dedicated managers. During the dire conditions of financial constraint, they did not receive a salary for five months. Karmaka himself had not received a salary for almost ten years.

When Karmaka left the hospital, one more blessing came. His application for Indonesian citizenship had been granted, without him even having to pay extra expenses! Astonishingly, in a move that evoked news coverage, Bung Karno (the intimate nickname given to President Sukarno) signed two approvals of citizenship by naturalization—one for Karmaka and the other for a Catholic priest from Bandung. These were the last two people to have naturalization papers signed by President Sukarno

CHAPTER TWENTY-FOUR

A WIFE'S SACRIFICE AND A NEW NAME

The issuance of Karmaka's citizenship was truly a blessing that boosted his spirit and enabled him to rebuild NISP. With heartfelt joy, he received God's gift of compassion. With his Indonesian citizenship, Karmaka could now legitimately lead NISP.

It had been more than a year since the special permit that allowed Karmaka to be the director of the bank had expired, and in the meantime, Karmaka had found an unusual solution that had kept NISP going. From Hong Kong, his father-in-law had suggested that Karmaka approach a prominent lawyer in Jakarta. Lie Nan-Tjing (who later changed his name to Rasyim Wiraatmadja) was a friend and confidant of Lim Khe-Tjie. Karmaka had asked Lie Nan-Tjing to be the president director of the bank.

Mr. Lie's acceptance of this request was very significant in the development of NISP. As a show of solidarity with Lim Khe Tjie and to demonstrate his sympathy for NISP, Mr. Lie had accepted the difficult job of taking over the helm at NISP despite its many intractable problems, which involved serious legal consequences.

Mr. Lie was not the only person to play a significant role during NISP's most difficult time. Peter Eko Sutioso, an attorney who had graduated from Pajajaran University in Bandung, was the first college graduate to work for NISP. As a college graduate with good grades, Peter made a surprising decision when he decided to join the troubled bank. He worked very hard to help Karmaka, especially in resolving legal matters, such as managing and resolving the issues that NISP faced as a result of its assets being under the control of other parties. For example, he made the necessary arrangements so that NISP could legitimately claim the confiscated properties as assets, an issue that had not yet been completely resolved yet, thereby strengthening the bank's capital structure.

Peter accompanied Karmaka wherever he went, including business trips to Jakarta, often four to five times a week. Sometimes they had to stay overnight and eat at roadside food vendors.

Peter's background as an activist in the Catholic Students Association of Indonesia was another significant contribution. Peter had close contacts with many prominent people in the community's Catholic society. There were many Catholic foundations with significant funds to manage. Having these types of clients gave the bank a more stable funding base, as the foundations tended to deposit on a long-term basis. Thus, the bank could make decisions based on the relatively predictable timing of the foundations' deposits and withdrawals. In contrast, personal funds were deposited or withdrawn unpredictably.

Karmaka would not forget the goodwill of the Catholic foundations in Bandung, especially when NISP was still experiencing difficulties in paying off the remaining severance pay of the laid-off employees, which amounted to 500,000,000 rupiah. For the bulk of the severance pay, Karmaka had to borrow a large sum from several parties, but he felt relieved that he was able to fulfill his promise to his former employees.

For security, the foundations asked for collateral when depositing their money with the bank. Karmaka racked his brains to figure out what more he could use as collateral. All the properties had been securitized. The only one that had not was his wife's house at Mesri Road No. 14 in Bandung, the house that she had inherited from her father. But how could he ask his wife to securitize her house? It was the only inheritance she had left that she could hold as a safeguard.

Upon hearing Karmaka's request, Lim Kwei-Ing objected; she begged Karmaka not to securitize her house, as it was her sole inheritance from her father. Yet Karmaka managed to persuade her; he explained that all these efforts were for the benefit of maintaining her father's bank. He also assured her that the loan would be safe and could be repaid. Eventually she gave in and signed the contract, putting the house up as collateral. Karmaka was very touched by his wife's sacrifice. He hugged her and wept. This is a prime example of Karmaka's compassionate and charitable nature. He sacrificed the family fortune for the sake of fulfilling his responsibility to pay the severance pay of the employees who had been laid off.

Lim Kwei-Ing's sacrifices did not stop there. To keep the bank running and to keep the house safe from foreclosure, his wife had to pitch in and help earn more money. Karmaka, who had promised not to receive any salary from the bank, was entangled in the problem of how to support his wife and four children. Taking into consideration the family's situation, as well as the problematic economy of the nation, Karmaka's wife proposed that she should work too.

Lim Kwei-Ing wanted to open a beauty salon. She could not afford to hire a hairdresser; therefore, she would have to become one herself. She asked Karmaka's permission to study cosmetics and hairstyling in Hong Kong. There, she could take courses on the most modern hair-styling inexpensively because her father and mother were residing there. While studying, she could stay with her parents.

Three months later, Lim Kwei-Ing returned from Hong Kong with expertise in cosmetics and hairstyling and, more importantly, the most modern styles. Immediately, she opened a beauty salon business, Star Salon, in her house. The tools she bought in Hong Kong were secondhand, but they were considered modern in Indonesia.

Star Salon became very popular, and the business grew quickly. On Saturdays and Sundays, Lim Kwei-Ing would work all day and all night, especially when brides made appointments to be made up and beautified before their weddings. On such occasions, Karmaka's wife would start the preparation at one o'clock in the morning. She would work on making up the brides and bridesmaids one by one until the morning of the wedding ceremony. Karmaka's four children, Parwati, Pramukti, Rukita, and Pramana, joined in and helped their mother.

"For twelve years my wife was the backbone of the family financial livelihood," Karmaka recalls. "All the family expenses were paid by the sweat and hard work of my wife. I did not bring home any money at all."

When Karmaka's friends praised Lim Kwei-Ing's skills, they would follow up with a question—why was the wife of a bank's president working so hard unnecessarily? They assumed that Karmaka had a lot of money.

Karmaka simply answered, "Oh, it's just her hobby."

He took pride in his friends' praise, but in his heart, he was crying, hiding his tears from public view. He did not want to expose the family's financial difficulties. Moreover, he did not want people to know that NISP was in such dismal circumstances. If they had known, people would have lost trust in NISP. He did not want others to know that his wife was the sole breadwinner for the family while Karmaka did not earn any salary. He wanted to maintain the bank's image.[13]

Slowly NISP Bank, which had already become a commercial bank, was revived. The issue of his Indonesian citizenship was resolved and Karmaka was able to lead and manage the bank officially. Karmaka saw his new citizenship status as a miracle. He had become almost hopeless, a sense that was fueled by the current political climate, unsure if he

---

[13]   Star Salon is still running as of the writing of this biography. It is kept as a memory of the past. Of course, Lim Kwei-Ing does not personally serve the customers any longer.

would ever get citizenship. He had neither the time nor the money to take additional measures. Meanwhile, President Sukarno's hold on power became shakier every day, and eventually, President Suharto replaced him. Why President Sukarno, in his last few days of power, bothered to sign the naturalization papers of a nobody by the name of Kwee Tjie Hoei from Bandung was anybody's guess. It was indeed a miracle of great mystery!

Karmaka would never have guessed that President Sukarno's signature would grace his citizenship papers. He was surprised when he learned about the doomed leader signing his document, along with that of a Catholic preacher, just before his downfall. "Thus, my citizenship papers really were a rarity," Karmaka says.

Karmaka was only too happy to comply when he learned of the regulation requiring Chinese emigrants holding Indonesian citizenship to change their names to Indonesian-sounding names. His wife changed her name to Lelarati. But what should he change his name to? How did the name Karmaka Surjaudaja come to be?

Karmaka approached a well-known painter and art instructor in Bandung, Mr. Barli. With delight, the artist gave him the name "Karmaka Surjaudaja." "Karmaka," Mr. Barli explained, means "has high fighting spirit and does not surrender in the face of difficult challenges." "Surjaudaja" means "strength from the sun" and can also mean "patriotism."

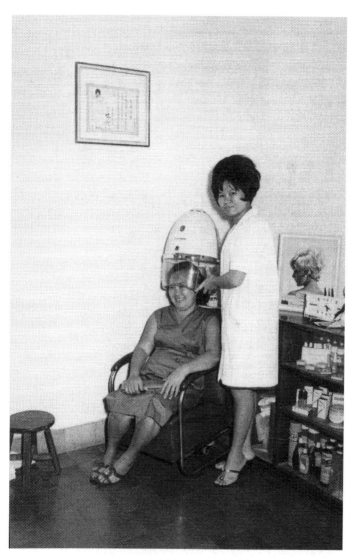

Lelarati working at Star Salon, which she founded in 1967.

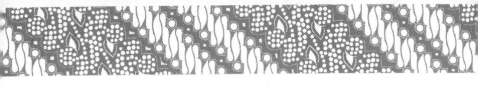

CHAPTER TWENTY-FIVE

DON'T SHOOT MY HUSBAND

After Karmaka successfully solved many of the problems NISP faced, he could now turn his mind to happier thoughts.

Unfortunately, this peaceful interlude did not last for very long. Just as he was enjoying the miraculous granting of his Indonesian citizenship, very disturbing news broke, throwing him back into an emotional turmoil. The new bank partner, who NISP was supposed to depend upon, was apparently not in good standing. The bank, which owned 43 percent of NISP's shares, had been ailing and was suspended by the Central Bank. Karmaka's emotions flared.

The partner bank had been borrowing money from NISP, to the tune of 46 million rupiah, through interbank loans in order to cover its liquidity shortfalls. Karmaka had often refused the request for these loans, to which the bank partner had always retorted with contemptuous words. "Why would I have agreed to the partnership if I cannot have the advantage?" he would demand.

Eventually, the big bank could no longer survive, and the authorities closed it. Karmaka was enraged.

Without much thought, he headed toward the partner's home. Loudly, he shouted, "You cheated me, didn't you?!" The disastrous loss of funds had hampered NISP's growth and now jeopardized its own survival; Karmaka's anger laced his words. "If the interbank loan does not get resolved, NISP will go bankrupt!" shouted Karmaka. "I would rather die than see NISP go bankrupt. I am willing to commit suicide. You are the one responsible for NISP's bankruptcy! Before I kill myself, I will shoot you first," he snapped. "Return the loan immediately, or I will shoot you!"

The bank owner's wife screamed, "Don't shoot! Don't shoot!" She told Karmaka that her husband was a good person, explaining that someone had swindled him, and she begged Karmaka for mercy.

Karmaka paused for a moment.

Seeing that Karmaka was willing to listen to their argument, the partner asked Karmaka to sit down and discuss the issue amiably.

"You said just now that I cheated you, yes?" asked the partner calmly. "Think back and search your conscience," he added. The partner reminded Karmaka of the first time Karmaka came to see him. Karmaka had asked him for help by buying the 43 percent of NISP shares at a high purchase price. "At that time, I did not bargain with you. I agreed right away to buy the shares," he told Karmaka.

The partner continued his story. "When you came to see me I knew just by looking at your eyes that your bank was in big trouble. Without asking any questions, I bought the shares because I needed to buy a new bank." In fact at that time, NISP had been carrying negative balance sheets and could practically be considered bankrupt. "I did not make an issue of it. I looked the other way, didn't I?" he added.

Karmaka was speechless. Deep down, he knew that what the partner was saying was true. *I have to be honest with myself*, he told himself.

The partner also admitted why he bought the NISP shares when he knew they were worthless at the time. "I needed to prove to people that my bank's finances were healthy and strong, capable of buying a significant part of NISP in the middle of the bank crisis," he said, revealing his tactic. Then he revealed that his own bank had been facing extraordinary difficulties itself at the time. He was unable to fulfill the minimal capital requirement imposed by Bank Indonesia; furthermore, he had to borrow money from NISP to make up the balance of daily interbank clearance shortfalls.

The partner, surrendering, dropped the pretense, "Now it's clear who was cheating whom. We cheated each other. There is nothing I can do now. If you still want to shoot me, go ahead. Shoot me right now—here, in front of my wife."

Karmaka stood transfixed and silent, thinking. In his inner heart, he knew that the partner spoke the truth. Realizing that, Karmaka let go of his anger and softened his stern expression. "Now then, how will this money be resolved?" asked Karmaka.

"Let's do this," the partner suggested. "You take all the shares, and we will consider the case closed."

Now it was Karmaka's turn to be confused. If he took over 43 percent of the shares, that would mean he would be burdened by all the obligations associated with those shares. If he did not take over the shares and shot the partner, the issues would still not be resolved. Moreover, if he did shoot the partner, it would result in turmoil in the community and the ruin of NISP's and his own good name. Thus, Karmaka found himself in a position in which, willing or not, he had to take the shares, along with the obligations of paying the debts associated with them.

Karmaka and the partner reached a consensus and prepared an agreement. The partner officially sold the shares to Karmaka's wife, who held the remaining 57 percent of NISP shares. Consequently, Lim Kwei-Ling would hold 100 percent of NISP's shares.

However, before they signed the contract, the partner requested an amendment to the agreement—Karmaka would buy his goodwill, in the amount of 10 million rupiah. Karmaka vehemently rejected this amendment, but the owner refused to sign the agreement without it.

"Please help me in my grim condition. We can't even go out to buy food," the partner begged. His wife joined in her husband's pleas. For several days, the partner did not dare to set foot outside his house for fear of the mobs of customers demanding withdrawal of their funds from his bank.

Karmaka, remembering the difficulties that he had faced in the past, was sympathetic to their plight. Yet where could Karmaka find the money to pay for the "goodwill"? Karmaka knew that if he confronted the partner about this issue, nothing would come out of it. Thus, with a heavy heart, he agreed to the amendment.

With this deal, his family would have 100 percent of the bank. Unfortunately, banking regulations prohibited bank ownership to be held by one sole owner. Karmaka had already anticipated such a situation. With the consent of his wife, he would set aside 5 percent of NISP's shares and offer them to an independent businessman prominent in the banking business, who Karmaka judged to be a good partner and a valuable advisor to NISP. This person had a strong conviction that NISP could be saved and would become a prosperous bank one day. "His belief," recalls Karmaka, "was based on the loyalty and hard work of NISP's personnel, who had been hardened by the experiences of the monetary crises and were prepared to face any challenges ahead."

But where would Karmaka get the money to buy the shares, along with their obligations? He had no choice but to obtain private loans, using his personal properties as collateral. It was all right, he decided. He would absorb the sacrifice again. He would do anything, as long as NISP could be saved.

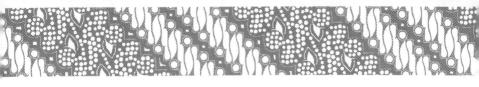

CHAPTER TWENTY-SIX

RIDING A VESPA TO FIND CUSTOMERS

With 95 percent of NISP's shares in the hands of his wife, Karmaka was even more determined to do his best to rescue and revive the bank his father-in-law had founded. Now his family had to bear the burden of practically all the bank's financial obligations to other parties.

As a result, Karmaka searched tirelessly for new customers, riding his Vespa scooter as if he were a mid-level employee, not the president of the bank. For Karmaka, riding his Vespa was a way to save money, as well as to navigate the heavy city traffic in the most practical way. With his Vespa, he could enter every corner of the city in a humble manner.

One day, he visited a store in Andir, the salted fish market district of Bandung. The store owner was his old friend, Yu Tjoan-Tek. As teenagers, the two had taken electronics courses together in a radio repair shop and also courses in car repair. Karmaka still remembered the name of the electronics school, Detroit, which was located in the main street, now named Jalan Riau, in Bandung.

Tjoan-Tek helped Karmaka a lot. Not only did he introduce Karmaka to his entire business network, he also offered to help Karmaka with any problems he might have. Even though Karmaka was the president of a bank, he was not yet considered to be a successful person. His friends took pity on him, as he was poor and still struggling for his bank business. Yu Tjoan-Tek was so sympathetic to him that he even let Karmaka use the living room of his house at Andir Market Road exclusively as an NISP office. Karmaka could use the living room from 10:00 a.m. to 2:00 p.m. rent free. Yu Tjoan-Tek also promised to introduce Karmaka to his brother, Yu Tjoan-Hok, who was working in a leading textile factory at the time. Yu Tjoan-Hok could work for Karmaka on a part-time basis and could ask the textile factory he worked for to become an NISP customer.

Over the course of his life, Karmaka encountered many kind people like Yu Tjoan-Tek. Karmaka often wondered how the world could be inhabited at once by so many good people and so many wicked people, such as the cruel manager of the textile factory who had humiliated him or the previous directors of NISP whose evil acts had almost driven NISP to bankruptcy. He felt blessed by God that he encountered people like Yu Tjoan-Tek and Peter Eko Sustiosa.

Thanks to Yu Tjoan-Tek and Yu Tjoan-Hok, in a very short time, NISP acquired 160 new businesses and individuals who were willing to become NISP customers. NISP continued to improve. By making payouts, which he could do by selling his wife's assets, Karmaka was able to gradually reduce NISP's debt and the private loans he'd taken to rescue the bank in the recent past. The bank's strength and resiliency would be proven later, when, in 1968 under the New Order government of President Suharto, another economic crisis would hit Indonesia, and NISP would not be greatly affected. In fact, while many banks collapsed during that time, NISP thrived. "Every day we heard of banks in crisis. I was worried that NISP might not survive. Thank God, NISP did survive," says Karmaka.

Thanks to Karmaka's hard work, he had successfully overcome the many challenges the bank faced, and in the middle of the crisis, NISP was reputed to be a responsible bank. NISP's strong reputation soon spread among the people at large. As a result, while many other banks were failing, NISP was flooded with new customers who had abandoned their shaky banks. In Bandung alone, at least six banks eventually went bankrupt. Of course their customers would need to find a more reliable bank.

With so many new customers coming in, Karmaka, Peter, and the rest of the NISP staff had to work extra hard. Although the employees had agreed that there would be no overtime pay, they worked day after day until eleven o'clock at night. They worked so hard for NISP because they believed that, when NISP prospered, they would enjoy the fruits of their labor.

As all the employees were so busy, the bank was shorthanded in several departments; it especially needed cashiers. So much money was coming in that there were not enough cashiers to handle it. "Even Peter and I had to join in to become cashiers," reminisces Karmaka, laughing.

Never in his life had Karmaka handled so much money; moreover, he had never seen money flowing so rapidly. Previously more money had been going out than coming in. Even though they worked hard and were tired, everyone was delighted and enthusiastic.

Not only did the customers come in person, but the phones also kept ringing. A great number of big customers asked for special services. "We had to visit their houses to collect the money," Karmaka remembers. Karmaka would ride his Vespa from house to house, usually with one of the employees in the backseat. He would drive the motorcycle while the employee would carry the money securely.

All employees came to work even on Saturdays and Sundays. New customers came flooding in, drawn in by the highly effective mouth-to-mouth advertising. The more people came to NISP, the more new customers were generated. The number of customers increased to such an extent that, after office closing time, some customers even came to Karmaka's house to hand him their money for next-day processing. Karmaka was good at interacting with customers. For example, when Karmaka dropped in to collect money, not only did he talk about the money and the bank, he also chatted with customers about their health and other tidbits of interests.

Karmaka was not satisfied with the bank's booming business. He realized that NISP still required more customers. Karmaka was very impressed by Peter, who continued to pursue his efforts to attract credible institutions and foundations to be NISP customers.

"That year, the growth of NISP was extraordinarily fast. I couldn't help but feel grateful to God," says Karmaka. He began attending church again; disappointed with God, he'd stopped going to church in 1964, after his younger brother was killed just right after graduating from medical school. At church, he expressed his gratitude to the Almighty for allowing NISP to survive and to grow with a speed beyond anyone's expectations.

Karmaka was also thankful for the strong commitment from all of his employees. The lack of overtime pay and salary raises, as well as the suspension of cost-of-living reimbursements, did not affect the employees' enthusiasm. Karmaka held many of his employees in high regard—people like *Pak* Peter, who later became director then deputy chairman; *Pak* Rasjim, who later became president director then chairman; and *Pak* Hakim, who later became director. Karmaka would always consider NISP employees heroes who would not be forgotten.

Moreover, Karmaka felt proud that, during his successful triumph over NISP's detrimental liquidity crisis, he had never received help from either Bank Indonesia or from strong business conglomerates buying his bank shares. Karmaka believed that God had blessed him with employees who were extraordinarily loyal, dedicated, and hardworking and with a strong fighting spirit and with tremendous cohesiveness. "If I told their story, nobody would believe it," says Karmaka.

Riding a Vespa to Search for Clients.

CHAPTER TWENTY-SEVEN

IMPRESSING THE JAPANESE

The flood of new customers during 1968 was truly a dramatic turning point in the history of NISP. From that point on, the conditions of the bank improved continuously, with no setbacks to slow it down. Five years later, in 1973, another decisive moment occurred due to the strength of Karmaka's personality, which again played a pivotal role in the growth of NISP.

At that time, NISP had just confiscated a building as collateral from a customer in Jakarta who had defaulted on his loan. Apparently, the same customer had also pledged the very same building to Bank Daiwa Perdania, a joint venture bank owned by a major ownership of Daiwa Bank (now Resona Bank) of Japan.

As such, Daiwa was also aiming to take over the building. However, since NISP's legal documents were better prepared than those of Daiwa, NISP acquired the building first. As a result, the owners of Daiwa Bank felt they had been treated unfairly.

NISP was able to act promptly solely because its personnel understood the local conditions well. "We were lucky to have *Pak* Rasjim Wiraartmadja on board as an active director. He was very clever in these kinds of matters," notes Karmaka. Rasjim was the attorney friend of Karmaka's father-in-law who had been asked to sit as NISP's director when Karmaka was still awaiting his Indonesian citizenship. As a local attorney, Rasjim knew the procedures well and was able to quickly acquire the building.

The CEO of Daiwa Bank in Indonesia was furious and said, in Japanese, "These Chinese used tricks to get it first." He spoke these words in front of Karmaka, never suspecting Karmaka would understand Japanese. Karmaka remained silent, even though he was very offended by the CEO's comments. Karmaka remembered well the three people who were representing Daiwa at that time. Two of them were the most senior people in Daiwa Bank Indonesia, Mr. Iwasa and Mr. Itasaka. The names stuck in Karmaka's memory, and they would later become intertwined in his life story.

Karmaka, an objective and fair person, remained positive in his thinking and ignored the offense. A person who thinks positively when offended is one who cares more about success than he or she does about personal feelings. Putting aside his feelings, Karmaka tried to determine how he could prove that he was not what the Japanese regarded him to be.

Karmaka told Mr. Iwasa that NISP only needed 8 million rupiah from the building, which had been assessed at more than 25 million rupiah. NISP would be willing to help Daiwa Bank recover its losses.

What was Mr. Iwasa's reaction? He was very angry. "This is nonsense! Let's leave," answered Mr. Iwasa, full of suspicions that NISP had somehow cheated in the transaction.

Karmaka maintained his positive thinking. He immediately auctioned off the asset, which was a well-located commercial building whose value was quite high. After subtracting the debt owed to NISP and the processing costs, 13 million rupiah remained that could be claimed by other eligible creditors. With the purpose of proving that he was not a crook as the Daiwa higher-ups had suggested, Karmaka asked to meet with Iwasa. But Iwasa refused, still thinking that the CEO of NISP had engaged in foul play.

Karmaka continued with his good faith and kept requesting a meeting with Iwasa. This time, he added that he had successfully auctioned off the property, and funds were available for Daiwa Perdania if the bank wanted them.

Having heard that, Iwasa was finally willing to meet Karmaka. As soon as Karmaka entered his office and at the moment of offering a handshake, Karmaka opened the greeting with, "*Mosi-mosi. Ohayo Gozaimasta. Watakusiwa Karmaka, NISP gingko no todori.*" (Hello. Good morning. I am Karmaka, CEO of Bank NISP.)

Iwasa was surprised at the unexpected Japanese greeting. "*Sodesnei, Anatawa nihongo wakarimassita des nei. Sumimaseng, dojo iratsiaimasita*" (I see that you understand Japanese. Pardon me, please be seated.)

After hearing that NISP could help process the 13 million rupiah for Daiwa Perdania Bank, Iwasa was very happy. He shook Karmaka's hand and said emotionally, "It has been twenty years since I began work in banking. This is the first time that I have met a true gentleman who is as decent and fair as *anatawa*[14]."

"Oh, it's nothing to me," Karmaka commented. "My parents always taught me to be an honest person, to respect others, to honor my elders, to be willing to work hard, and to be loyal to my company. They always said that the key to running a successful company is trust," said Karmaka.

Unexpectedly, Mr. Iwasa began to open up and shared with Karmaka that, beginning next year, the Indonesian government would issue a regulation prohibiting foreign banks from owning branches outside of Jakarta. Daiwa Perdania Bank, he explained, was looking for a local partner to serve customers outside of the capital city, Jakarta. "Right now, six banks have already applied. I suggest that NISP do so as well. Who knows? NISP might be chosen," said Iwasa.

Still speaking in Japanese, Karmaka expressed his appreciation for the offer. But Karmaka admitted that he would be embarrassed to apply, since NISP was only a very small bank.

---

[14] *Anatawa* is a polite form of "you" in Japanese.

Hearing Karmaka's humble reply, Mr. Iwasa said it was better not to think so. "The Japanese very much value people who are gentlemen, people who are honest and fair like you," said Iwasa.

At first, Karmaka was doubtful that Iwasa's words were genuine. Perhaps the Daiwa CEO was just making small talk in response to Karmaka's help. Karmaka nevertheless sent the application without expecting much.

Apparently all those words were not just idle conversation. Within a week, Karmaka received a call from Mr. Iwasa. "Congratulations, Karmaka-san! Daiwa has chosen NISP as its sole partner," Iwasa informed him.

Karmaka admits that he immediately shed tears. "I was moved. It felt like a dream that NISP was chosen as partner of Daiwa, one of the largest banks in Japan." Daiwa was the first joint venture bank in Indonesia. That NISP should be a part of this endeavor was truly beyond his expectations.

Karmaka had no idea how to conduct a joint operation, but he immediately contacted Daiwa Bank and expressed his gratitude. He also gave his oath to be a loyal, honest, and hardworking partner. Karmaka expressed the hope that the partnership would bring progress for both Daiwa and NISP.

At the next meeting between the two banks, Daiwa asked NISP to submit the conditions NISP desired. Karmaka responded to this inquiry using humble words. "We are a small bank. It would not be proper to ask for conditions of any kinds," answered Karmaka. But Daiwa insisted that there should be an agreement in black and white signed by both sides in order to avoid future disputes.

On their end, Daiwa wanted one person to serve as technical assistant to NISP who would be in the office daily. Daiwa also asked NISP to reopen branches in Semarang and Surabaya, two major cities aside from the capital city of Jakarta, as early as possible, since many Japanese companies were located in Central and East Java.

To the first request, Karmaka had no objection, since it had to be so. Karmaka had a long-term view that, through the technical assistant, NISP could learn a lot from Daiwa. As for the second request, Karmaka was delighted. He had wished for a long time to reopen NISP's branches in Semarang and Surabaya. That doing so was a requirement for Daiwa was a pleasant surprise.

NISP was unable to open the two branches because of lack of capital. Now, with the request from Daiwa, Karmaka had the opportunity to propose several funding conditions to Daiwa.

Karmaka submitted NISP's requests, which the bank called "555", similar to the name of a well-known cigarette. The triple five was significant. NISP asked Daiwa to provide a loan of US$5 million, for a period of five years, at 5 percent interest per year.

Hearing the request, Mr. Iwasa was surprised. "The loan amount is too big. It would not be possible," said Mr. Iwasa.

Karmaka explained that the fund, in large part, would be used to reopen the two bank branches Daiwa had requested. Specifically, the funds would buy a commercial building for the office, office equipment, and a house to serve as the residence of the branch manager. The rest would be for joint financing of common operational expenses. "Anyway, all the expenditures would have to be cleared by Daiwa's technical assistant. We are not going to take advantage of you for our own interests," assured Karmaka. In addition, the regulations of Bank Indonesia obligated NISP to continue strengthening bank capital.

Daiwa evaluated Karmaka's requests. The bigger bank was attracted by the proposal that the US$5 million US loan would be a private loan, secured by Karmaka's wife's NISP shares. As a private loan, the utilization of the fund would be more flexible but judicious and would still be under the control of Daiwa's technical assistant.

"Eventually all my requests were granted," says Karmaka with great delight, as if the granting had just occurred.

Karmaka still remembers the first person who was assigned to be Daiwa's technical assistant at NISP. Chiomori-san was a very good person who was able to work well with the people of NISP.

From that time on, NISP started to grow fast and became more stable. That Karmaka's positive thinking, honesty, and fairness had engendered the trust of a foreign bank was an important starting point for NISP's journey to the success it would know far into the future.

CHAPTER TWENTY-EIGHT

THE DEATH OF A HERO

The progress that NISP had achieved eased Karmaka's burden, especially his feeling of responsibility toward his father-in-law. It became clearer that the bank Lim Khe-Tjie had founded would not go bankrupt. Year after year since 1968, NISP's reputation had been getting better and better. Over time, the people and businesses of Indonesia recognized NISP as a very prudent bank. The bank was very careful in giving out loans, and the customers were generally very loyal because of the bank's trustworthiness. This loyalty and the bank's trustworthiness would once again be proven in 1997 when Indonesia would be hit hard by the devastating Asian financial crisis.

A Dutchman initially started NISP on April 4, 1941, on the eve of World War II. The bank was registered for business under the colonial Dutch government with the name of N.V. Nederland Indische Spaar & Deposito Bank, abbreviated as NISP. However, the owner did not dare to open the business with the uncertainty brought on by the looming war in Europe, which might affect economic conditions in the colony of Dutch East Indies. Furthermore, a year later Japan invaded and occupied Indonesia for three and a half years. When the war ended with the surrender of the Japanese to the allied forces in Indonesia, a four and a half year struggle for Indonesian independence followed. With the final departure of the colonial government, the environment was not conducive for a Dutchman to operate a bank.

The Dutchman happened to be a friend of Lim Khe-Tjie. In 1948, the Dutch friend offered to sell the license to Lim Khe-Tjie for 5,000 gulden, the Dutch currency. The price was only for the license, since NISP had no other assets of any kind at the time.

Lim Khe-Tjie asked his wife to consider the offer. His wife was enthusiastic because she wanted her husband to run a more stable business. In the city of Bandung, the husband and wife were known to be in the business of making and selling tofu. To acquire the banking license, they sold the tofu business, as well as Lim Khe-Tjie's jewelry. The couple had immigrated from Hokjia, Fujian, China to the Dutch East Indies. In Bandung, they owned and lived in a house at Mesri Road, number 14, where they ran their tofu business.

After acquiring NISP's license, Lim Khe-Tjie changed the name of the bank to an Indonesian one. The name had to be formulated in such a way that, when abbreviated, it would match the abbreviation of the Dutch name. Even though the Indonesian name—PT *BankTabungan Nilai Inti Sari Penyimpanan* (The Value Essence Savings Bank)—was rather long and difficult to remember, Lim Khe-Tjie insisted that the bank use it; the name was shortened to PT Bank NISP. The true founder of NISP, Lim Khe-Tjie transformed the license into an operational business.

The first NISP office was a rented room above the Java Book Store, located at the famous shopping area of Braga Street in Bandung. Lim Khe-Tjie asked the previous license owner, his Dutch friend, to serve as the director, while Lim Khe-Tjie himself was the commissioner. Indonesia was using the Dutch banking system of two boards in a company—the board of directors and the board of commissioners.

Lim Khe-Tjie was skilled in managing and growing the bank. He used a strategy wherein he asked influential people in major cities to act as the bank's agents. He was even able to recruit a well-known person who later became a very famous minister in the government. The agents, who were paid by commission, were to get as many customers as they could to open saving accounts and make deposits.

In four years, Bank NISP showed fast growth. However, in 1952 the Dutch director had to leave Indonesia because he could no longer get a permit to stay in the country. Lim Khe-Tjie did not have enough schooling to fulfill the requirements of a director. He had only finished elementary school. Therefore, he promoted an NISP employee who had a higher educational degree to replace the director, while Lim Khe-Tjie remained the bank's commissioner.

The legacy of the Dutch director was that he created the image of NISP as a bank with a strong administration. He applied great care and caution in the practices of banking. Indeed, the Dutch were well known all over the world for being very professional in the tight running of financial businesses.

Two years later, in 1952, NISP had opened up many branches with substantial accumulation of saving deposits. However, since NISP was licensed only as a savings bank, the utilization of the capital was very limited. Luckily, Lim Khe-Tjie came up with the idea of establishing another bank, which would be licensed for commercial lending, to better channel the accumulated deposits of NISP for higher productivity. Therefore, he established PT *Sejahtera Bank Umum* (SBU). NISP's channeled its excess funds to SBU to be used in commercial lending.

The office of SBU was in the same building as that of NISP but on a different floor. The director for SBU was the younger brother of the director appointed to lead NISP.

SBU experienced rapid growth. As a result, the office became too crowded. SBU moved to a new office building located on Suniaraja Street, the confiscated property of an NISP customer with bad debts. Much later, after continuous fast growth, the main office of the SBU moved to Jakarta.

However, SBU's fate was much worse than that of NISP. Not long after Lim Khe-Tjie went to China to pay homage to his ancestors in 1959, SBU was somehow sold without his approval.

As to the founder of these institutions, Mr. Lim Khe-Tjie's fate was heartbreaking. His departure to China with his family, meant to fulfill the Chinese ritual of honoring the burial place of his ancestors, extended far beyond the time period he'd ever imagined it might when his return to Indonesia was denied. During his twelve years of absence from Indonesia, many unfortunate events took place. SBU was gone. NISP suffered many disastrous events and was on the brink of disappearing. When Lim Khe-Tjie finally returned to Indonesia, NISP was just beginning its recovery. Fate denied him the chance to witness the unbelievable feats Karmaka achieved to bring NISP to its present glory, which would have brought Lim Khe-Tjie great pride and consolation with regard to the bank he'd founded in 1948.

In 1977, Lim Khe-Tjie was diagnosed with a liver disease, which later developed into cancer. During his sickness, Lim Khe-Tjie stated in his last will that, when he died, he wished to be buried in Indonesia. All the family members knew that Lim Khe-Tjie loved Indonesia very much. Therefore, after a discussion of who would care for him in Bandung, one of his daughters, Karmaka's wife Lelarati, was entrusted to care for him in his last days.

Enduring his sickness, Lim Khe-Tjie had, at long last, returned to Indonesia. Lelarati cared for him well. After seven months, Lim Khe-Tjie passed away on August 17, 1978—Indonesian Independence Day. His death on this heroic date was a reminder that Lim Khe-Tjie had been one of the heroes in the struggle for Indonesia independence, a miraculous coincidence,

He should have been buried at the hero's cemetery park, but he had lost this privilege when he'd declined the honor of Independence Hero, stating that his Dutch friends would have known that he had betrayed them, passing on the important information they'd shared with him to the Indonesian Army during the war for independence.

Lim Khe-Tjie had requested that he be buried in the Chinese cemetery in Cikadut, Bandung, and it was there that Lim Khe-Tjie was finally put to rest. Six years later, he was followed by his wife, who was buried at his side.

CHAPTER TWENTY-NINE

SERVICE TO THE NATION

The long period of stability in the growth and development of NISP after the 1970s gave Karmaka much-needed breathing room. Just at the right period, he had time to spend with his family. His four children were becoming teenagers and needed guidance from their parents.

During this period, Karmaka spent his time building his children's character with activities such as swimming, drawing, horse-back riding and the Outbound program. They were coached in building self-esteem, having courage to face challenges, being cautious in decision-making, learning self-defense, and many other things. At times he was able to accompany his children during their art lessons as well. Karmaka also took the children for walks through the villages surrounding Bandung with the purpose of teaching the children to love nature, while at the same time recognizing the living conditions of the village communities.

During the walks along rivers, rice fields, and woods, Karmaka encouraged the children to observe how the farmers worked and how the community members earned their living. "I wanted my children to value the work of the farmers, who are the source of livelihood of the society," Karmaka explains. With the walks, Karmaka also wanted to teach the children to love their country. "All of these lessons," he adds, "were very important and would serve as their foundation later in life."

When his eldest son, Pramana, completed high school, Karmaka sent him to the state medical school of Pajajaran University. Pramana graduated and became a medical doctor. The second child, a daughter named Rukita, later graduated and became a dentist. They both served as civil servants.

The third child, a son named Pramukti, was sent to study banking and finance in the United States, as was the fourth child, a daughter named Parwati, who studied accounting and finance in the United States.

Much later on, Karmaka invited all four of his children to help at NISP. Pramana and Rukita served as members of the supervisory board, and Pramukti and Parwati were appointed members of the executive board. The participation of the family members in the bank business enriched the core strength of NISP as each family member had accumulated varied work experiences before joining NISP.

Before helping NISP to develop its human resource department, Pramana had made his contributions to society. After graduating from medical school, he was assigned to community service. At that time, regulations decreed that medical graduates could not continue their studies to become specialists before completing community service. The length of the community service depended on the location the service would be conducted in. In the city, the medical graduate had to serve for five years. However, if the service was in a remote village, it would only last one year. The regulation was meant to increase the availability of medical services in the poorer areas of the nation, as doctors tended to choose to practice in the cities and towns.

Pramana enthusiastically chose to serve in a remote area, both to tend to the health of the poor and to spend a shorter time before studying a medical specialization. He was assigned to a very isolated, underdeveloped, and remote area in the southern corner of West Java. The area had never been effectively ruled during the 350 years of Dutch colonization.

Pramana became a "victim" of the remoteness of the place. When his one year of service was complete, he was not permitted to leave the village because there was no one to replace him yet. Consequently, Pramana had to extend his stay for another year, no longer as an obligatory service fellowship but as a volunteer. At the end of his second year of service, the village still had no replacement, and he was asked to stay for another year. He served for three years, two of which were as a volunteer, in the isolated areas south of the city of Cianjur. Aside from there being no one to replace him, other reasons motivated the villagers to ask Pramana to remain with them for so long—the community loved him dearly. The village insisted that he stay and petitioned the authorities to retain him.

During this period, Karmaka had occasion to visit his son. He was proud that his son was willing to work in a village with no electricity, no clean water, and no paved roads, reachable only by narrow trails. To serve the community, Pramana had to commute on either a motorized dirt bicycle or on horseback. For Karmaka to see his son, he had to travel over seven rivers with rapid streams which, in the rainy season, were very treacherous to cross.

Karmaka eventually reached the village named Cidaun Selatan where his son, the doctor, lived. This village was in the middle of a jungle inhabited by many kinds of snakes. The villagers did not dare to kill snakes because snakes were revered as gods. They believed that killing a snake would bring disaster upon the village. The area was also well known as a center of mysticism and practitioners of black magic.

Karmaka could not bear to see his son serving in a village where conditions were so desolate, especially when he saw the "house" in which his son lived; it was more of a shack than a house. However, Pramana vowed to serve there, in spite of the discomfort and the many challenges he faced. He did all he could to keep the villagers healthy. Karmaka was moved with pride. He helped his son by buying him a motorized dirt bicycle and supplying him with medicine, medical equipment, and other expendables.

Pramana survived three life-threatening incidents during his stay in Cidaun Selatan. The first one occurred when he attempted to cross a river on a bamboo raft. A large wave overtook the raft and capsized it. The villagers were astonished when they found his dirt bicycle without him. They immediately began a search, and Pramana was found caught among the dense bushes unconscious and with a bleeding head wound.

The second incident occurred when Pramana was riding his dirt bicycle. Out of nowhere, a python crossed his bike's path. Pramana could not stop his bicycle in time and ran over the python. The python immediately wrapped itself around his body and began squeezing him. Luckily, a powerful *pawang* (magical animal charmer) came to save Pramana from the snake's constriction. The snake eventually disappeared into the jungle.

The third incident occurred when Pramana was helping a shooting club that had just arrived from the city for a hunting trip. In the middle of the hunting trip, a torrential downpour caused a landslide. The hunting group, led by Pramana, was trapped inside the jungle for three days. Their food was depleted, so they killed a snake to eat.

The news that the party had killed a snake spread among the community. Not long after the hunters had returned, angry villagers surrounded Pramana's house. They shouted and demanded that Pramana come out to be killed for violating the villagers' tradition of honoring the sacred snakes.

Luckily, many of the prominent figures in the village were willing to speak on Pramana's behalf. They told the villagers that Pramana was a good person who had helped the local communities greatly. But between the groups for and against Pramana, no compromise could be reached. The threat of fighting among them was looming. Fortunately, the security apparatus from the city intervened, and the issue was finally settled.

Pramana performed tremendous services for the villages of Cidaun. He served not only in the areas of medicine and health care but also in social and religious affairs. He helped to repair many mosques and schools. Pramana provided health care for free. Karmaka financed the purchase of whatever materials he needed to help the communities. "It was quite a large amount of money that I spent monthly, but I was glad I could help the poor communities," Karmaka remembers.

Karmaka's generous financing was later expanded when Pramana helped to build and widen the roads in the villages and paid school fees for children who could not afford their elementary and high school education.

The community of Cidaun would long remember one event. Four young village girls who had applied to study nursing were rejected and came to Pramana crying. Sympathetic with their struggle to fulfill their dreams, Pramana used whatever means possible on their behalf. Eventually, the four girls were accepted into the nursing school. News spread among the villagers of Cidaun that Pramana was a hero of the villages. "Long live Pramana!" shouted the people of Cidaun.

"I am very proud to have a son with such a big heart, who is so selfless in his service to society and who loves his homeland, Indonesia, so strongly," says Karmaka. "It's no wonder; he is the grandson of Lim Khe-Tjie, a hero of Indonesian independence." The proud father remembers his son once telling him that he did not want to achieve any less than his grandfather had for the nation.

It was no surprise that, when the time came for Pramana to be replaced by a new doctor, the parting ceremony was attended by a huge number of villagers and dignitaries who came in from the seven villages of Southern Cianjur. Moreover, the head of the West Java Department of Heath made a concerted effort to attend, even though he was not feeling well. He was escorted to the ceremonial place by riding on the back of a motorcycle driven by his guard, since the roads could not yet accommodate automobiles.

Karmaka attended the ceremony, intending to bring his son home afterward. He shed tears when he saw banner after banner praising his son: "Long live Dr. Pramana!" Villagers distributed pamphlets during the ceremony that read, "We, the people of the seven villages of Southern Cianjur present our gratitude and highest reverence to Dr. Pramana. We wish so much that our beloved Dr. Pramana would settle here with us. We offer our assurance of a livelihood, security, and a place to live."

The head of the Department of Health was in tears and told Karmaka that it was the first time he had witnessed such an emotional scene. He asked Karmaka how he'd instilled in his children such a strong dedication to the community.

"I noticed that many of the villagers wept when Pramana left the villages behind," Karmaka remembers.

Karmaka's late first son, Dr. Pramana, MD MBA.

CHAPTER THIRTY

AGAINST ALL ODDS

As Karmaka Surjaudaja reached forty years of age, NISP was dynamically stable, and the bank faced no major challenges during the next eight years. It was as if NISP were a ship that was finally sailing in tranquil waters with no storms threatening to sink it. Even though there were some choppy waters here and there, the ups and downs only served to enhance the experience and maturity of NISP leadership. This period was in stark contrast with the previous twelve years when the ship had almost sunk several times in the stormy waters. Luckily, when the ship was confronted with the ferocious storms, Karmaka was still in his youth and had inexhaustible strength and energy of body and mind to overcome the challenges and prevent the ship from sinking. The Chinese legend *Ba Xian Guoa Hai* (Eight Immortals Crossing the Sea*)*, which tells of seven gods overcoming dangers and successfully crossing seas, could symbolize these dangerous twelve years.

During the eight tranquil years that followed, NISP grew steadily. Even though the bank was not one of the biggest in the nation, it was very well recognized as a prudent and conservative bank with loyal employees and customers. Karmaka's children also developed rapidly. Pramana and Rukita graduated from medical and dental schools

149

respectively. Pramukti, Parwati, and Sanitri completed their education with MBA degrees in the United States.

The end of the eight years of stability appeared to be a turning point of a different kind for NISP. Calamities inflicted upon the family forced Karmaka to think hard about how to prepare his successors to ensure NISP's stability and prosperity in the future. His preparations would later prove to be quite necessary.

The first calamity was the death of Mr. Lim Khe-Tjie, Karmaka's father-in-law and the founder of NISP, who succumbed to liver cancer in 1978. The second calamity involved Karmaka himself. Karmaka, at age 44, was diagnosed with liver cirrhosis and was told that he had only five years left to live. This news prompted Karmaka to make a strategic decision that would affect the future of NISP.

Karmaka's liver cirrhosis was discovered when it was already well advanced. However, if his father-in-law had not died of liver disease, he would have never known that he himself was ill. The passing of his father-in-law prompted his wife to urge him to have his liver examined since he had often complained of being tired, a common symptom of liver problems. The laboratory results were positive for liver cirrhosis.

From that time on, Karmaka had to visit a medical laboratory regularly for blood tests. One time, the laboratory made a mistake. Karmaka's wife, Lelarati, concerned with the quality of laboratory testing, was inspired to open up a clinical laboratory business herself, so that Karmaka would be tested weekly in a facility that ensured him highly reliable results. The business, Biotest Clinical Laboratory, thrived due its strong reputation for data reliability and on-time services. Lelarati—assisted by her daughter, Rukita; her daughter-in-law Anna Tjandrawati (Pramana's wife), who was a medical doctor specializing in pathology; and her son-in-law Januar Sudarsono (Rukita's husband), a medical doctor specializing in radiology—led the business. Biotest would later expand to several regions of the country.[15]

---

[15] As of the writing of this biography, Biotest has sixteen offices in Bandung, Jakarta, and Surabaya. In 2010, Biotest celebrated its thirtieth year in

As for Karmaka's liver ailment, Lelarati did not immediately believe that her husband's diagnosis of liver cirrhosis was correct. The couple went to consult a liver expert, a university professor in Jakarta. After his examination, the professor came to the same conclusion: Karmaka was suffering from advanced liver cirrhosis that was untreatable. Hearing the confirmation by the liver expert, Lelarati broke into tears. "God, why is this happening?" she cried.

Liver cirrhosis cannot be treated or reversed because the liver cannot repair cirrhosis by itself, nor can it do so with the aid of medicine. Moreover, in Karmaka's case, the cirrhosis was diagnosed to be cancerous. Karmaka would eventually be told that he had only five years to live.

From that point on, Karmaka's concentration was divided. On the one hand, he had to focus on maintaining NISP's progress—a progress that had taxed his body and soul during the last twenty years. On the other hand, he had to start thinking about how to cure his liver cancer and save his life. While he was still living, he had to focus on speeding up the development of his children to take over the bank one day. Karmaka went to work daily as usual, but his mind was on his wife and children, who were very upset by the doctors' diagnosis.

While searching for ways to cope with his disease, Karmaka also kept contemplating the future of NISP should he pass away after five years.

Pramana had just completed his three year community medical service in South Cianjur and was continuing with his studies as a medical specialist in Semarang, Central Java. Thinking that staying in Semarang would keep him away from his father, who would not live much longer, Pramana followed his parents' advice and dropped out of school after only nine months. Instead, he studied business in Jakarta, going for an MBA in human resources management.

Karmaka considered that Pramana could receive his MBA in two years and, for the remaining three years of Karmaka's life, he would

business.

groom Pramana to run NISP. Karmaka made the right decision. Pramana would later restructure and upgrade the human resources of NISP in accordance with the demands of the changing era. Moreover, Pramana would also establish an educational and training center to raise the employees' capabilities by training and developing all levels of employees. In the beginning, the center was very small. It would later be upgraded with sophisticated equipment, training facilities, and accommodations.

Pramana is also remembered nationally as the initiator of Indonesia's softball team and a developer of outstanding players. He was an expert in team building in sports. In fact, during Pramana's time as coach, the poorly performing softball team of Indonesia finally won in the ASEAN (Association of South East Asian Nations) Olympics. Pramana would later recruit many of the national softball athletes to become NISP employees.

Karmaka also decided to send his second son, Pramukti, and second daughter, Parwati, to the United States. At that time, both had just completed high school in Indonesia. Karmaka asked the two to study hard so as to graduate speedily and complete their studies before his impending death. *There is still time*, thought Karmaka.

While the children were completing their search for knowledge and skills related to banking management, Karmaka continued to steer the bank and to find ways to escape his impending death. In 1980, two years after the diagnosis of liver cirrhosis, Karmaka discovered that there was a world-renowned liver expert in the United States—Dr. Fenton Shaffner of Mount Sinai Hospital in New York City. An acquaintance put him in touch with Dr. Shaffner.

Accompanied by Lelarati, Karmaka flew to New York City. After a thorough examination, Dr. Shaffner informed Karmaka that he had been misdiagnosed. "There is definitely no cancer," Dr. Shaffner told him. Nor was cirrhosis Karmaka's liver problem. Rather, the doctor determined that Karmaka was suffering from non-A, non-B hepatitis.

Biotest Clinical Labs, Jakarta 2010.

Karmaka (left) with Dr. Fenton Schaffner &
Dr. Henry W.P. Lim.

CHAPTER THIRTY-ONE

PREPARING FOR GRADUAL TRANSITIONS

U pon returning from Mount Sinai Hospital in New York City, Karmaka went back to managing NISP full time, though his body tired easily. While thinking of ways to nurture himself back to health, he bore witness to the progression of his children's education. Pramana, who had stopped being a physician, was diligent and keen at studying his business management classes. In the United States, Pramukti and Parwati studied diligently and lived frugally. They lived in school dormitories, walked to classes, and relied on public transportation to get around. He did not want to spoil his children, as so many other well-to-do Indonesian parents had when their children studied abroad.

Karmaka told the children that he had only five years to live. He encouraged them to study harder and faster in order to come back and help him run the bank. To develop their interpersonal skills, Karmaka also reminded them to attend self-improvement classes such as those offered through the Dale Carnegie Institute, which his good friend, Simon Rusmin, PhD, recommended. Karmaka considered lessons, such as those Carnegie taught in *How to Win Friends and Influence People*, important for candidates in management and leadership, particularly his children, who he imagined would take over the leadership of NISP when the time came for him to leave.

While continuously monitoring the progress of his children's education, Karmaka kept himself busy managing the bank and regularly checking his liver function through laboratory testing.

Suddenly, after about a year, the test results became very bad. All his liver function indicators were getting drastically worse. The test results diverged greatly from normal reading ranges.

Thus, in 1982 Karmaka went back to New York City to see Dr. Fenton Shaffner again. The results of Dr. Shaffner's examination were even more shocking. Karmaka's liver disease was definitively worse than it had been when he'd received his first diagnosis. Karmaka was now diagnosed with primary biliary cirrhosis (PBC), a disease for which there was no cure at the time. The illness meant that his liver would eventually stop functioning. Dr. Shaffner explained that the many possible causes of PBC included extraordinary stress, smoking, or drinking. Since Karmaka did not smoke or drink alcohol, the stressful life experiences Karmaka had gone through in the past twenty years since were the presumable cause. The stress that had contributed to Karmaka's disease might even date back to his childhood and youth when his family was poor and he had to do physically and mentally demanding jobs to support the family.

All indications showed that Karmaka had severe PBC. The doctor told him that searching for other physicians or treatments would only be a waste of time and money. Generally for a terminal case like this, doctors would advise their patients to live their lives as best they could without stress until the arrival of their eventual deaths.

Karmaka was dazed and confused. How could he live without stress? His children were not yet ready to take over the business and replace him. Every day, Karmaka prayed that his life would be extended a little longer, at least until the children had graduated from school. In the meantime, he kept encouraging them to study diligently so as to complete their schooling earlier.

Karmaka's children proved their devotion to their parents. Within four years, the eldest three had obtained their MBA degrees—Pramana's in human resources management, Pramukti's in banking and finance, and Parwati's in accounting with cum laude. Sanitri was the only one who remained in school.

Yet even in his worsening health condition, Karmaka felt that he should give his children more experience before they took over. If the prediction that he had five years remaining of his life proved true, he had only a few years left to groom his children and increase their business acumen. Under his management, NISP had been progressing quite well, and capable and loyal employees led essential departments.

Therefore Karmaka put his "remaining two years" to good use, having his children earn work experience outside of NISP. Pramukti worked at Daiwa Bank, which placed him in different departments where he could study best banking practices and broaden his financial knowledge, as well as learn how to interact with different people of diverse cultures. He worked in Daiwa offices in New York, London, Hong Kong, Osaka, and Tokyo. Later, Daiwa Bank even granted him a scholarship to attend the International University of Japan in Niigata, Japan, where he studied international relations; this proved to be a valuable experience for Pramukti's future career.

Parwati also accepted employment prior to joining NISP. A well-known accounting and management consulting firm, SGV Utomo, which was under the leadership of the famous Utomo Djosodirdjo, in Jakarta, Indonesia, offered her work in the office. SGV Utomo later merged with a giant American company, Arthur Andersen Consulting, where Parwati got practical experience of great value, specifically in the areas of planning and finance.

While waiting for the maturation of his children before his "year of death," Karmaka was escorted by Lelarati to China to try different remedies for his illness. Karmaka figured it couldn't hurt to try other remedies and treatments, since there was no other means of healing that Western medicine could offer. Incidentally, Karmaka knew many people in China, including his former students from Nan Hua in Bandung. Karmaka's friends introduced him to many doctors who practiced traditional Chinese medicine in Beijing, Shanghai, and Hangzhou. Karmaka took traditional Chinese herbal medicines and, more importantly, he diligently practiced the breathing exercises of Qigong and Tai Qi Quan (Tai Chi). The experts in China said that the breathing exercises could, at the very least, extend his life.

Considering that he still needed to look after NISP for the time being, Karmaka could not stay in China for extended periods. He traveled back and forth on average three to four times a year, staying in China for ten to fifteen days each time.

During all this, NISP continued to operate smoothly, and Karmaka's children were getting valuable experience in banking and finance. The five-year deadline Karmaka's doctor had given him was approaching quickly; four of those years had passed already. Karmaka still had one year left to prepare the new leadership of NISP.

Karmaka (left) with Simon Rusmin, Ph.D.

CHAPTER THIRTY-TWO

THE NEXT GENERATION

Five years had gone by; the deadline for Karmaka's death had come and gone. Miraculously, there were no signs that Karmaka was dying at all. Karmaka had been suffering from this deadly disease while his mind had been preoccupied with the future of NISP. His spirits were still high, and he was still physically strong enough to go on with his daily work. Karmaka remained active as NISP's CEO. It was possible that the breathing exercises of Qi Gong and Tai Qi Quan, which he practiced intensively, had sustained his physical strength and slowed down the progression of his illness. Karmaka's condition, much better than the prognosis, had made it possible for his children to get a wide range of experiences abroad before returning home to serve on the boards of the bank.

In 1987, Karmaka's liver functions test readings suddenly worsened. Immediately, Karmaka was admitted into Boromeus Hospital in Bandung. However, the doctors could not do anything except advise Karmaka to stay home for better care. Karmaka summoned his son, Pramukti, to return home immediately to serve on the board of NISP.

On September 1, 1987, Pramukti arrived from Japan. Once in Indonesia, he was placed from one bank department to another to study and understand the operations of each department that would later fall under his charge.

Eventually, on January 9, 1989, Pramukti was installed as the director of NISP. This coincided with Karmaka's plan to change the organization and leadership of the board. The change was prompted by the death of one of NISP's commissioners, Sarono SH, and by the retirement request of Rasjim to move from his position as executive director to that of commissioner.

Three years later, Parwati, who was working for SGV Utomo Consulting, was also called in to take the position of director.

In 1997, fifteen years had passed since Karmaka had received the "verdict" about his death. Karmaka again was able to oversee a reorganization of the bank structure. This would be recorded in NISP's history as a successful generational transition of leadership from father to sons and daughter. In the new management structure, Karmaka relinquished his executive role to his children; he served as chairman of the board of commissioners, along with other senior NISP leaders, including Eko Sutioso, who was deputy chairman. Karmaka's wife, Lelarati Lukman, became a member of the board of commissioners along with their first son, Pramana, and daughter, Rukita. Their second son, Pramukti, became the chief executive officer, and their second daughter, Parwati, served as deputy CEO. Furthermore, many other young, smart, capable and loyal individuals were promoted to join NISP's upper management.

With his children at the helm, Karmaka witnessed the growth of NISP into an even larger and stronger bank, due to progressive changes in business management. In 1992, two years after his children took over, NISP obtained a foreign exchange license, a move previously opposed by a few key NISP leaders who were concerned with the complexity of operation and the risks it entailed. However, Pramukti and Parwati successful convinced the opposition, arguing that not being a foreign exchange bank would actually make it harder for NISP to compete in the existing banking environment.

Moreover, in 1994 Pramukti and Parwati proposed another strategic change to restructure NISP into a publicly listed company. The proposal was accepted, and initially, 20 percent of NISP shares was made available to the public to strengthen the bank's capital. Pramukti and Parwati foresaw the intensified competition in modern banking and knew that, without modernization, the survival of NISP would prove difficult in the future.

In the middle of global banking competition and acquisitions, Karmaka received news that Daiwa Bank faced severe financial problems, caused by a big loss in treasury dealings that the executive of their New York office had conducted. As a result, the bank had to be restructured by the Japanese government, and the institution's name was changed to Resona Bank.

Karmaka remembered well that it was the partnership with Daiwa Bank in the past that had functioned as a stepping stone bringing progress to the growth of NISP. Also, it was Daiwa that had provided Pramukti the opportunity to receive training in banking practices immediately after his graduation from college. In fact, the institutions had discussed striking a deal for a long-term commitment between Daiwa and NISP by signing a strategic alliance between Karmaka and Sumio Abekawa, Daiwa's president director. Of course the plan failed to be realized with Daiwa's downfall.

Karmaka had found peace in his heart, despite having to continually monitor the condition of his health. The children had quickly gained experience in the banking business, and NISP progressed rapidly. Karmaka felt blessed that he was still alive and that his health remained sustainable in 1996. He continued practicing Tai Qi Chuan and periodically visited China for counseling on his health. He maintained his activities as NISP chairman and continued to help develop his children's business expertise.

Soon eighteen years had passed since Karmaka was first diagnosed with liver disease and told that he had only five years to live. At the end of each year ever since, Karmaka felt miraculously blessed that he had been given yet another year. So it was when the year 1997—the disastrous year of the Asian monetary crisis—arrived. Even in such a dire situation, Karmaka felt optimistic that, in that year, he would still be alive and NISP would still be moving forward.

However, the Asian Financial Crisis, which started in Thailand, proved to be deadly—it soon spread all over South East Asia. In July, Indonesia was still not affected, yet the feeling among Indonesians, especially those in business circles, was that of apprehension. The government announced that the foundations of the Indonesian economy were still sound, but people believed this less and less. While Indonesia's economists were still hotly debating whether to change the open floating currency exchange system to a fixed exchange system, the crisis inevitably arrived in Indonesia. The exchange rate of the Indonesian currency (rupiah) to the US dollar plummeted lower and lower every day. To those who were in the banking business, it felt like they were being pushed closer and closer toward the edge of a cliff and that, at any time, they would fall over the edge.

Karmaka and his children were on high alert. They had to anticipate, watch for, and react to every probability and possibility. The whole of NISP management was put on red alert, and so were the operators of all other businesses. Ideas and discussions abounded, and businesses tried various steps. Transactions and funds moved quickly.

During this stressful period, Karmaka was working in his office when suddenly blood began gushing from his mouth. Apparently, the blood vessels of his stomach had burst, causing massive internal bleeding. In a very short time, Karmaka became unconscious.

First NISP shareholders meeting after going public, 1995.

CHAPTER THIRTY-THREE

DAILY ANXIETY

Karmaka was rushed to the intensive care unit of Boromeus Hospital in Bandung. The examination showed that blood vessels in his digestive tract had broken in seven places. Normally, blood from the digestive system ends up in the liver, where it is processed. Since Karmaka suffered from cirrhosis, or hardening of the liver blood vessels, blood from his digestive track reached a dead-end obstruction in the liver. The blood collected in the blood vessels of the digestive tract and gradually distended the vessels to become bubbles, which grew bigger and bigger from day to day. The medical term for this condition is *esophageal varicosities*. Almost all liver cirrhosis patients experience the breaking of these bubbles, which then results in bloody vomit and stools. For Karmaka, this had happened six times before, and he was able to recover from it. But this time, the ruptures occurred at the junction between the esophagus and the stomach. Bleeding in this section is difficult to control and is the cause of death among most sufferers of cirrhosis.

Along with performing surgery to close the broken vessels, doctors administered an immediate blood transfusion. To the staff and workers of Bandung NISP office, the grave atmosphere of the Asian monetary crisis became a secondary concern as they turned their attention to the safety of their leader. Without being asked, the employees stood in line to have their blood tested. Those people with compatible blood types donated their blood to save Karmaka. Fourteen people donated their blood, including Pramana. The blood was transfused while Karmaka was still unconscious.

Fortunately, the doctors kept his bleeding under control by pressurizing a balloon along the esophageal tract. At that point, the decision to have a liver transplant was the only option. Still unconscious, Karmaka was flown directly to New York City via Singapore. Karmaka's wife and most of their children, including two in-laws who were both medical doctors, accompanied him during the flights. They were slightly relieved to see that Karmaka had started to regain consciousness during the journey.

With high hopes, Karmaka's children requested that the hospital provide immediate care for Karmaka. However, the doctors informed them that they could not perform a liver transplant right away. "There is a long waiting list for a donor's liver. The wait could be as long as one year," the doctor explained. Indeed, many patients with organ failure, including liver failure, die because no donor is available. Moreover, Karmaka's type B blood was very rare; thus, finding a match in the United States would be difficult.

Pramana, the medical doctor, begged again and again to have his father given priority. "We cannot," answered the doctor. "Sorry, but there are rules in the United States. Whoever is first on the waiting list will be the first to be attended to," the doctor added.

There was no other choice but for Karmaka to stay in New York City while waiting his turn. When that would be was a big unknown. He could wait a week, a month, or even a year.

Time passed. Days turned to weeks, weeks turned into months, and no donor was available for Karmaka.

At least his condition was no longer critical. The bleeding of the digestive tract was under control, but the potential that it might occur again loomed large. His blood vessels could burst again in the same or other places.

In the meantime, the Asian monetary crisis was worsening by the day. Rumors abounded in the banking sector, as if a high magnitude earthquake had stricken the banks. News of bank closings was heard almost daily. Today "A" bank was closed, tomorrow "B" was heard to be shaky, and other banks were leery, waiting for their turn. Lists of failing banks were circulated among the business community, creating a loss of confidence among bank customers, who started closing their accounts and withdrawing their deposits.

What happened to NISP? None of the family members were in the bank offices of Jakarta or Bandung. All of them were in New York City caring for Karmaka. Meanwhile, the bank directors updated them continuously, telling them of the aggravated situation in banking and the economy in general. However, the family could not personally and directly observe and assess what was happening in Indonesia and see how bad the threat to NISP was. Even though internally NISP's financial condition was still intact, the external conditions could be a substantial threat.

While Karmaka was lying in an intensive care room of a hospital in New York City, his mind was transported far away to his motherland, trying to analyze what could be happening in Indonesia and guessing what terrible things could have befallen the bank that he had fought for with his life.

Finally, Karmaka decided that all his children should return to Indonesia. He did not need to be attended while waiting for an unpredictable period of time for a liver donor, while they were needed more at the sites in Indonesia, even though the problems could have been handled by those left behind. NISP had capable directors, but it would be different, Karmaka thought, when the family leadership was around to boost their morale and confront the crisis together. Karmaka did not want another disastrous outcome like that of the

Indonesian monetary crises of 1965 when the currency was devalued a thousandfold.

The children refused. They insisted on staying with Karmaka to ensure that he would be properly treated during his hospitalization.

But Karmaka was firm, and he pretended to be very angry. "I would rather die here and now than have you all stay!" threatened Karmaka.

The children discussed the situation among themselves. They knew their father's personality and character. They knew that their father was determined and might kill himself, the one thing that they would never want to happen. The children also didn't want their father to be angry.

Therefore, they fulfilled Karmaka's wishes. They all cried, hugging their father farewell. Lelarati, the children, and the in-laws departed for Indonesia. Karmaka felt relieved that someone he trusted would be taking care of NISP during such a critical situation. He was glad that, eventually, all his children were willing to return home.

Unknown to Karmaka, the children had decided that the youngest child, Sanitri Surjaudaja, would stay in New York. She was assigned to stay with him at all times, without Karmaka's knowledge, until Karmaka had his liver transplant, and she would be reporting on his condition and progress to the family in Indonesia.

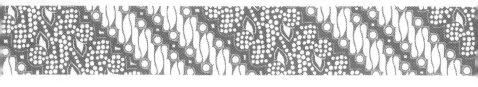

CHAPTER THIRTY-FOUR

DECIDING TO DIE

After his family members had left for Indonesia, Karmaka was by himself in Mount Sinai Hospital in New York City. Every night, Karmaka contemplated his life. His thoughts wandered through his life's journey—from his childhood to his teenage years when he'd been his family's breadwinner; from rejecting the temptation of wealth in exchange for the love of his future wife to the responsibility his father-in-law had bequeathed him by asking him to save NISP; from the seemingly intractable difficulties that had befallen NISP to the triumph of rescuing, sustaining, and finally helping the bank to blossom.

His thoughts also wandered to his children, whom he had guided in developing their characters and enhancing their knowledge and experience so that they could take on the leadership of NISP. He thought also of his faithful wife, who had given him the courage to confront desperate circumstances; he thought of her efforts in supporting the family by learning hairstyling in Hong Kong and opening a beauty salon. Persisting with her entrepreneurial spirit, Lelarati had successfully created a medical clinic laboratory business with the help of their first daughter and son-in-law with branches established in many major cities of Indonesia.

His thoughts wandered to the condition of his body. When the doctor had predicted that he would not live more than five years with his liver disease, he had accepted this pronouncement. And yet, here he was, lying on a hospital bed, eighteen years after receiving the verdict of death.

His mind wandered again; he contemplated the prospect of getting a liver donor. Would he be able to find a donor in time? His illness had come to the most critical moment, yet the waiting period was so uncertain. He had to wait for someone with a matching blood type to die. A person's death could not be predicted. However, one could decide when to die.

Karmaka came to the conclusion that he was ready to die. He had seen NISP become prosperous. He had seen that his children and wife would be capable of carrying on with their lives without him. He had completed his life's duties on earth. Realizing how difficult and how unlikely it was that he would get a liver donor, Karmaka decided that he would rather die than trouble other people. Karmaka did not want to be a burden to his wife, children, and in-laws—all of whom had sacrificed so much for him.

After contemplating all day long, nightfall came. The hospital became quiet, and all the nurses returned to their stations. When the sleeping bell sounded and lights dimmed, Karmaka came to his final decision—he was going to commit suicide.

He proceeded to unplug the tubing connected to his arms, nose, and feet, including the blood infusion tube. He also shut off his oxygen supply.

Afterward, he sat on the bed and bent forward at his waist, pressing down on his stomach. Karmaka thought that, by doing this, he could burst the ballooning blood vessels along his digestive tract and stomach. By stopping his blood infusion, he thought he would bleed out and finish his life in peace and that the nurses who arrived in his room the next day would find him dead.

After performing these acts, Karmaka felt that his belly began to distend and believed that he had been successful. However, before reaching his death, he wanted to pray.

To pray, Karmaka needed to get down from his bed. He wanted to kneel on the floor in front of a window overlooking a wall. He wanted God to accept his soul. He told God that he wanted to kill himself because he didn't want to trouble the people he loved any longer. Also he didn't want his wife and children, whom he had inconvenienced for too long, to witness the moment of his death. At the end of his prayer, Karmaka asked for forgiveness for two grave sins he had committed during his lifetime. The two sins had been very difficult to forget even at that moment. These sins followed and haunted him wherever he went. Maybe someone else would not consider these to be sins, at least not grave sins, but to Karmaka, the two sins were serious transgressions against God.

His first sin was abandoning God. He had stopped going to church in 1964 because he was disappointed in God. For a period of 10 years, he had sacrificed his life by working in a textile factory to finance his younger brother's medical education. He was hanging on to the hope that when his brother became a doctor, he would have sufficient income to reciprocate by realizing Karmaka's dream of attending electrical engineering classes at Bandung Institute of Technology. For all those years, Karmaka and his mother had attended church faithfully and consistently, praying to God for his brother's speedy graduation from the medical school. Eventually, his brother graduated cum laude and was ready to begin his specialization. But God abruptly took his brother's life in a fatal car accident.

His second sin was laying off three thousand bank employees as a consequence of the government's devaluing the currency a thousandfold. NISP had been on the verge of bankruptcy, and he'd had to lay off the employees in order to save NISP. The country had faced a serious economic crisis, and closing the majority of NISP's branches had been the only way to rescue the bank. Nevertheless, Karmaka felt a tremendous guilt, especially since he was very close to his employees. His guilt was so entrenched that it was hard to erase from his memory. He had always imagined how dreadful it was for workers to be laid off and how difficult their lives would have subsequently been.

He confessed his sins, whimpering in a pitiful voice and imagining that God was there listening to his every word. The longer he prayed, the more he felt that he was indeed talking directly to God. Without realizing it, he made a request to God to grant him a new liver within the next three days. At that moment, he forgot that he was confessing his sins. At the end of his prayer, he realized that he was on the floor next to his bed in the hospital in New York City.

When he finished with his weeping prayer, Karmaka climbed up onto his bed. He combed his hair, tidied the bed sheets and pillows, and smoothed his clothes. He had tidied everything so that when he was found dead the next morning, everything would be immaculate and in place.

When all was done, Karmaka turned off the light and covered his body with the blanket. He closed his eyes, anticipating his death. From there on, Karmaka had no recollection of what happened next.

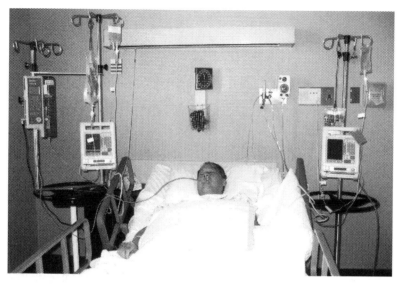

Karmaka in a coma for nine days at Mt.
Elizabeth Hospital, Singapore, 2005.

Karmaka (frontmost) practicing Tai Chi.

CHAPTER THIRTY-FIVE

THE BLESSINGS OF REPENTANCE

The death that Karmaka had so meticulously planned and prepared for did not arrive after all. After lying on bed all night long, he did not remember what happened, not because he had died but because he had fallen fast asleep.

As dawn approached, he was awakened by a loud noise. A loud scream from a nurse ended his slumber. Having seen all the tubes for infusion, transfusion, and oxygen supply disconnected from Karmaka's body, the nurse screamed as loudly as she could. She ran through the corridors screaming for help. In split seconds, seven nurses rushed into Karmaka's room.

"All the nurses scolded me and treated me in an awfully disapproving manner," says Karmaka.

The nurses did not understand why he would do such a thing. "If you had died, we and the hospital could be indicted in court," a hospital staff member told Karmaka.

Karmaka had not suspected that the consequences of his attempted suicide would be so serious. He thought he would die without troubling anyone anymore. His wife, children, in-laws, and other people need not be troubled by worrying and caring for him. He did not realize that he would jeopardize the nurses, the doctors and even the reputation of Mount Sinai Hospital itself.

"We would all be in trouble for what you did," said the hospital staff.

Karmaka immediately regretted what he had done and that he had not taken such serious consequences into account. Yet Karmaka did not want to admit that he had attempted suicide. He was afraid that his admission would complicate his hospital stay. Therefore Karmaka racked his brain to find an excuse; even a flimsy excuse would do.

"I was dreaming that someone was trying to kill me. Therefore, a fight ensued. I unplugged all the tubing connected to my body so that I could fight the killer," Karmaka claimed.

"Nonsense!" they responded. "Impossible," they added.

The nurses proceeded to tie Karmaka's body, arms, and legs to the bed. That was the procedure they had to follow for unruly patients like Karmaka. Patients who unplugged their life-support systems were considered to have a psychological problem. There was no other choice but to restrain Karmaka to his bed.

Karmaka was very angry that he was being treated as a person with mental illness. Karmaka asked not to be restrained. However, the nurses did not want to take any risks. If Karmaka were to attempt to take himself off life support again, the nurses would be blamed for negligence in their duties. They might even face litigation in court. "All the doctors and nurses have been working so hard to save you," said one of the doctors. "Why have you done such a foolish thing that will get us into trouble?"

Karmaka realized that what he had done was wrong and earnestly apologized. He also insisted that he had really dreamed that someone was coming to kill him. Karmaka promised not to do such a thing again, and he begged to not be tied to the bed. "If I am tied up this way, I might as well die," pleaded Karmaka.

After some discussion, the staff agreed to untie Karmaka. However, they decided that one nurse would have to guard him. From there on, Karmaka was guarded twenty-four hours a day.

In the morning, Karmaka wanted to see the color of his stool after emptying his bowels; would it be reddish black due to internal bleeding? He was sure it would be because he had bent over and had exerted pressure on his abdomen the night before. "Apparently, it remained yellow," he mumbled. Every day, Karmaka made the inspection, but he did not see what he expected to see.

On the third day after his failed attempt at suicide, at 10 o'clock in the morning, Karmaka received unexpected news. "We have a donor!" a nurse informed him "You have to be prepared immediately for the transplant."

Karmaka was shocked and surprised! Feelings of gratefulness and delight overwhelmed him. He was grateful to God, since this meant that God had always been there for him and had listened to his prayers and request. He was also delighted and grateful that the blood vessels in his stomach had not burst as he had wished, which God had also willed.

The hospital staff quickly took Karmaka to the operating room. An Asian person had been involved in a fatal accident, and thus, a new liver was unexpectedly and suddenly available. After a quick examination, the donor liver was deemed perfect and was set aside for Karmaka. The liver donor was only thirty-one years old.

By the time Karmaka entered the operating room, he felt calm and peaceful. He knew that he was being saved. He asked the hospital to not inform his wife and children so as not to trouble them. He felt relieved that his wife and children would not be aware of the operation so they would not be apprehensive.

Unbeknownst to Karmaka, during this entire time, his youngest child, Sanitri, had been in the hospital hiding from him in the guest room and following the progress of the operation. It was she who gave the family the news that Karmaka was getting a donor liver and that the transplant would take place immediately.

That night, Karmaka regained consciousness. He was relieved that his life had been saved. He found himself alone in the intensive care unit of Mount Sinai Hospital in New York City. When he examined his surroundings, looking to his left and to his right, Karmaka was astonished to see his youngest child, Sanitri, beside him.

Noticing that her father was aware of her presence, Sanitri ran to his side and held his hand. Tears poured from her eyes. She revealed that she had been with him the entire time instead of returning home with the family. She had hidden herself from her father in the guest room. As such, she was able to follow her father's progress and report to her mother and siblings in Indonesia.

Sanitri told her father that she had already delivered the news of the successful transplant to the family at home. "They are all on their way to be here now. They will arrive tomorrow," Sanitri reported.

Karmaka felt grateful. He was grateful that his prayers had been answered. He was grateful that he had been given a longer life. He longed to see the continuing development of NISP, to which he had dedicated his life. He had prepared his children to take over and continue the enterprise. So many heroic and beloved individuals had pledged their loyalty to NISP during the bank's darkest moments. He expressed his gratitude to the staff and workers of NISP whom he regarded as heroes for rescuing NISP from oblivion.

Three days after the liver transplantation, Karmaka was to be moved from the intensive care unit to a regular hospital room. Karmaka refused. He wanted to stay in the ICU for at least one week to make sure he was well. However, his request was rejected since he was well enough to move into a regular hospital room. The ICU was to be used by the patients who needed it most.

Karmaka got out of bed supported by two nurses, one on each side. He was about to be seated in a wheelchair so he could be taken to his new room. After standing up, Karmaka felt that his body was strong enough to walk. He asked the nurses if he could walk by himself without their support or that the wheelchair. A doctor, seeing that Karmaka was reluctant to be assisted by the nurses, asked, "What happened?"

In English, Karmaka asked to walk by himself.

"No, no, I am sorry!" the doctor replied. But then the doctor asked, "Can you?"

"Yes! Sure I can," responded Karmaka.

And so Karmaka's request was granted. He was allowed to walk by himself but had to be escorted by the nurses. Should he fall down, the hospital would be held responsible.

Karmaka was able to walk one, two, three, and up to thirteen steps.

At that moment, one of the doctors who was responsible for his care shouted, "Stop! Stop! That's enough!"

Karmaka stopped, and all the nurses and doctors who had seen Karmaka take the thirteen steps applauded him. Karmaka felt his spirits rise.

"You are Superman," said one of the nurses, after seeing him walk by himself just three days after surgery.

Karmaka was elated once more when he arrived at the convalescent room; his wife and children were already gathered there to receive him.

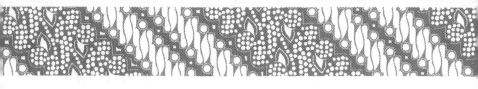

CHAPTER THIRTY-SIX

CRISIS AND DEDICATION

Leaving the ICU after the liver transplant, Karmaka did not experience any worrisome or serious complications. Furthermore, his condition improved steadily during his hospital stay.

After his discharge from the hospital, Karmaka was not allowed to go back to Indonesia. He was required to reside near the hospital for at least three months should something unexpected happen to his new liver.

Since his recovery was smooth and uneventful, Karmaka asked his wife and children to quickly return to Indonesia. The Asian monetary crisis was getting worse. Many banks were facing liquidity problems due to massive customer withdrawal of funds. The economy was becoming more chaotic. The rupiah exchange rate was in free fall, and interest rates rocketed sky-high. The political situation was in a mess. Mass demonstrations continued to erupt with no sign of stopping. The unity of the government began to show cracks, and President Suharto's position was becoming increasingly untenable. With his country in such an unstable and calamitous condition, Karmaka thought it would be better to have his wife and children return to Indonesia rather than stay with him in New York City. He asked that only his youngest child, Sanitri, who had been there incognito, be with him.

Three weeks after his liver transplant, Karmaka moved to an apartment not far from the hospital. However, before the three-month stay was over, Karmaka decided to return home to Indonesia. He was compelled to do so for good reasons. Firstly, he felt that he was strong enough and did not expect any sudden complications with his new liver. Secondly, he was very worried about the condition of NISP, as the economic, political, and security situation of Indonesia was deteriorating from day to day.

When Karmaka eventually landed in Indonesia, he was moved by the warm welcoming party that awaited him. He wept with joy. His welcome party was even larger and warmer when he arrived in his hometown of Bandung, where hundreds of people gathered at the airport. The staff, workers, and customers of NISP waved their hands to greet Karmaka upon his homecoming. They held up posters and banners to celebrate his arrival. Their exuberant welcome brought Karmaka a lot of joy and made him proud of the working relationships built on deep loyalty and kinship that he nurtured at NISP. This atmosphere was the one that he had been longing for and could not bear to be away from for too long.

Now that he was back in his homeland, Karmaka could see for himself how dangerous and menacing the unpredictable economic and political atmosphere was to NISP. Bank runs occurred everywhere leading to bank closures. Rumors circled that a bank would be next to close, and thus, its closure became a reality. The banking sector of the economy was very fragile and in a state of panic.

Two days after his arrival, Karmaka received a call from a customer he knew well. *Pak* Solichin, the owner of Banda store, opened the conversation with an expression of sympathy. "I feel sorry for NISP," *Pak* Solichin began. "NISP got run too."

"Is that right?" asked Karmaka, suddenly panicked.

"Yes," replied *Pak* Solichin. "A lot of people are crowding the entrance to NISP bank. I myself wanted to get in but could not. I have been here for the last two hours, but I am still outside."

Karmaka immediately took action. If NISP were run like that, it would certainly collapse. No matter how strong a bank was, it could not withstand being rushed by a panicked crowd. Karmaka immediately made phone calls to NISP's leadership. However, none of the managers answered the phone. Nobody answering the phone indicated that the situation was very serious. Karmaka was getting more nervous because he was not sure if the managers or even he himself could handle a massive deposit withdrawal of that magnitude.

Even with his health in a precarious state, less than five months after the liver transplant, Karmaka forced himself to go to Bank NISP. His driver drove him toward the bank. From a distance, he saw many people crowding the front of the building. He was very worried; if every one of them withdrew his or her funds, NISP would be ruined. The closer he got to the bank, the faster his heart beat. The car arrived at the bank, and Karmaka got a better look at the situation. People could not get in because all entrances to the bank building were jammed with people.

Karmaka was impatient. He got out of the car and tried to get through the crowd and into his office. His legs were shaking as he pushed his way through. Karmaka prayed for the safety of NISP and all of its employees. The frightening memory of the rowdy customers in 1966 (when the currency experienced massive devaluation) came back and chilled him to his bones.

In the midst of the crowd, Karmaka caught sight of an NISP customer that he recognized, a notary public. Karmaka knew that he was recovering from a stroke that rendered him unable to speak. He signaled, indicating that he wanted to speak to Karmaka. Karmaka approached him, and together they pushed their way through the crowd. Eventually, with much difficulty, they entered the building. His notary public customer wrote on a piece of paper what he wanted to say. Karmaka wondered if he was going to withdraw all his money.

"I am angered by the poor service of NISP," the customer wrote." "I have been standing on line for three hours, and I still have not been served." He wrote more, "I wasn't even asked to be seated."

Karmaka sympathized with his plight, knowing that the customer had difficulty standing upright because the strength of his legs was also affected by the stroke. How could he be allowed to stand for three hours? Karmaka was frustrated by the run. He also suspected that the service at NISP had deteriorated after he left for medical treatment in the United States. Wasn't NISP well known for its excellent customer service? Didn't NISP employ hardworking and loyal employees? How could things have gotten so bad? Those were the questions that occupied Karmaka's mind at the moment.

To calm the customer's anger, Karmaka invited him to sit in a special room. Karmaka earnestly apologized for what had happened to the customer. Then, he asked him politely how much of his money he wanted to withdraw.

After being treated with courtesy and respect, the customer pointed to his assistant who was standing beside him. His assistant was carrying a sack which looked like it was more than half full with something. He motioned to the helper to open the sack.

"I came here to deposit this money," he wrote.

Karmaka was shocked. This was fantastic! In the middle of a run, someone was actually making a deposit. This kind of person deserved the best treatment. During a run, a deposit is like a blood infusion for a bank. The person making a deposit could serve as an inoculation against a bank run.

Thus, Karmaka valued this customer greatly and he was more than ready to treat him with the utmost respect and courtesy.

The customer asked his assistant to empty the sack containing the cash. "Here is all my money. 60,000,000 rupiah worth," he wrote.

Eventually, Karmaka got a chance to sit down, and he slowly realized that the crowd of people standing in line in front of NISP was not there to take money out from NISP. They were standing in line to deposit their money. This was no bank run! This was a deluge that would flood NISP with cash. This was not a disaster but a blessing! In the middle of devastating bank runs, NISP was being "run" by new customers who were making cash deposits. In fact, this was the money that people had withdrawn from the other banks that had closed or were considered to be no longer viable.

Karmaka was tremendously relieved. NISP had, in fact, gained strength at a time when other banks were facing difficulties. This was because of NISP's image as being a very conservative and cautious bank. Karmaka could hardly believe that so many people were making deposits into his bank. It was strange that people were willing to stand in line for hours to make deposits. This meant that a crisis of distrust had actually befallen many banks. This was the economic situation at that time.

Karmaka encouraged the bank staff and workers to be patient and to keep up their hard work. He then supplied all employees with food and drink. They worked until late at night and then returned the next morning to repeat it all again. They were tired but delighted, stressed but proud. Every day the bank took in floods of cash, and Karmaka's recovery from his surgery suddenly seemed to accelerate. Similar events occurred at NISP banks in Jakarta.

When the political crisis reached its peak in May 1998, street rioting started to explode. Crowds, orchestrated by certain political groups, started to invade, plunder, and ransack Chinese businesses. Looters even started to burn houses, kill people, and rape women. They threatened the ethnic Chinese minority's economy and society, both physically and psychologically, endangering their bodies and souls and their properties and lives.

In this dangerous situation, the employees of NISP in Jakarta took action that touched Karmaka. During the rioting, destruction, and looting, the employees closed down the NISP office building at Gunung Sahari Street in Mangga Dua district. All the NISP employees gathered outside the bank building. They stood vigil in front of the building and were determined to protect the bank, even if that meant their blood would be spilled. Their bravery was priceless. The street of Gunung Sahari was the epicenter of the rioting, destruction, and looting. Nevertheless, all NISP employees blocked the rioters by linking their arms and standing in front of the building. The rioters, approaching in large numbers, could not get through the wall of employees' bodies. Their defense was too solid.

The employees also used verbal persuasion in defense of the bank. Some rioters were determined to destroy the building, and they came forward with sharp weapons. The employees convinced them that, if NISP were destroyed, the losers would be the little people like themselves. The employees said that they were defending the bank on behalf of the common people. Deterred, the rioters backed off.

In the aftermath of the rioting seven banks in the Gunung Sahari area and thirty-two banks in the Mangga Dua district were totally destroyed. Only NISP was saved. The building didn't receive so much as a scratch during the rioting. It was spared because of the tenacity of the NISP employees. The employees, who were ready to die, were safe and fine. No employees were injured or hurt during the rioting.

The stories of NISP employees' struggle would live on forever and be imprinted onto the souls of Karmaka and all the generations of NISP employees and leadership to come. This spirit of NISP was worth emulating by everyone, and this spirit is what made Karmaka realize that NISP was very special indeed.

After the rioters left their path of destruction, Karmaka received many questions from colleagues and fellow bankers. How much money did Karmaka spend to ensure that NISP's building stood safe and sound? How many military tanks were brought in to protect it? How did he force the employees to form a human barricade in front of the bank?

In response to those questions, Karmaka always answered with pride. He explained that the bank had not spent a cent, no tanks guarded the building, and there was no coercion of the employees as many had imagined. What saved NISP, Karmaka would say over and over, was the dedication and loyalty of all the NISP employees.

The grateful communities surrounding the NISP office also contributed to its salvation. Community members, thankful for the attention NISP paid to the community, had voluntarily joined in on the protection of NISP's buildings. The company's mission statement was clearly not just words. NISP would be an honorable member of the community; the bank honored this commitment. NISP added value to the communities in which NISP offices were located.

Later, everyone recognized that NISP was one of few banks that escaped the Asian monetary crisis without a scratch. People also recognized that NISP was a bank that one could trust. NISP received various awards, such as best bank in Indonesia, best managed company, and more.

At that time, as the interest rate indicator of Bank Indonesia itself had reached a high point of 70 percent, all banks were posting ridiculously high interest rates. However, NISP maintained its interest rate on loans at a rate lower than the market rate and even lower than the interest rate for saving deposits. NISP realized that the inflated rates were a momentary phenomenon and that following the crowd would jeopardize the long-term goal of NISP—to be a bank that could gain the trust and loyalty of customers, a bank that could establish long-term relationships, rather than seasonal ones.

CHAPTER THIRTY-SEVEN

INTERNATIONAL BANKING RECOGNITION

A person who has undergone a liver transplant like Karmaka has to take medication daily, sometimes five times a day. The medications are very potent and have harmful side effects that have to be countered with other equally potent medications. One such potent medication was an immunosuppressant used to prevent rejection of the new liver by the body's immune system, thus allowing the liver to function in synchrony with all the other organs.

As a consequence of taking so many medications, cancerous tumors developed in Karmaka's right kidney. Moreover, the cancer had spread to his bladder. In 2002, five years after his liver transplant, Karmaka needed to undergo major surgery on his kidney.

Karmaka went to UCLA Medical Center in Los Angeles, California, to see a doctor who was an expert on kidney surgery for patients who have had liver transplants. It was there that Karmaka's right kidney was removed. From that time on, Karmaka had to live with only one kidney. To treat the spread of the tumor to the bladder, Karmaka had to make frequent visits to Los Angeles to remove the tumors. To remove the tumors, the doctor inserted an instrument through Karmaka's urinary tract to access the bladder. After the procedure, for four months, he had to go to Singapore regularly for chemotherapy to kill any tumor cells that might still remain.

While vacationing on the outer island of Lombok with his family, Karmaka injured himself. He fell from his bed when he hurriedly woke up to catch the flight home. He broke his femur, and the pain was excruciating. Nevertheless, he forced himself to walk with a pair of crutches.

When Karmaka arrived in Bandung, the doctor who treated him recommended that he be on bed rest for three months and restrict himself from moving around. Karmaka, who had always been very active and needed to be mobile, could not accept that recommendation.

Two weeks later, Karmaka tried to walk using only one crutch and found that he could. A week after that, he tried to walk without crutches and discovered he could do so too. In three weeks, Karmaka was already able to walk normally. He didn't need to stay in bed for three months as the doctor had ordered. Karmaka held the conviction that the mind could overpower the body, as proven by his extraordinary recovery.

After Karmaka's right kidney was removed, his left kidney was not functioning well, which led to heart failure. One day, Karmaka suddenly found it difficult to breath; then he vomited blood and fell unconscious. He was immediately taken to the emergency room of Boromeus Hospital in Bandung and stayed there for nine days. Fortunately, the doctors were able to get the heart condition under control, but the function of his left kidney remained critically weak and was getting worse by the day.

Karmaka had two choices for treating the kidney problem—kidney dialysis or a kidney transplant. Eventually, he decided to undergo kidney transplantation.

Karmaka was destined to witness the progress of NISP, especially under the leadership of his children. He was also glad to have witnessed the hiring of smart new employees, who helped to speed NISP's progress. Thanks to his children's leadership and their new assistants, NISP increased in value, reputation, prestige, and trust, both inside and outside of Indonesia.

As NISP started to experience unbounded prosperity, however, another unexpected calamity befell the family. Karmaka's eldest son, Pramana passed away in Bandung. Pramana had taken his children, nieces, and nephews, and children of the bank's employees out in the wilderness for Outbound training. He got into a car accident and was killed, along with the program instructor. Fortunately, all the children were safe and unharmed.

With this loss, Pramana's tremendous empathy and unbounded selflessness in caring for and helping others became all the more poignant. His dedication as a civil servant during his obligatory postgraduate medical service in the remote areas of West Java, his leadership of the softball team that won the ASEAN competition, and his guidance in human resources training and development left a deep impression on those whose life paths had crossed with his.

The legacy Pramana left behind in building NISP's human resources left a lasting impact on the bank's modernization and refinement of the strong, traditional corporate culture of NISP. This corporate culture is defined by unity, hard work, and loyalty to the company as one big family. A banker who sat on NISP's board of directors representing the International Fund Corporation (IFC), a member of the World Bank, was very impressed by NISP. "In my tens of years of banking experience covering many nations, I have never seen a culture among the employees such as that of NISP," he stated.

During the Asian monetary crises, Regent Pacific Group (RPG) from England also participated in strengthening NISP in addition to the IFC. At that time, international financial institutions were avoiding Indonesia and other Asian countries affected by the monetary crisis. Nevertheless, the two financial institutions came to NISP's aid. RPG even dared to offer a low interest rate loan to Karmaka's family, the majority shareholder, with the rights of share conversion to strengthen NISP. Later, the loan was converted into a 33 percent share of NISP.

Apprehension arose when the director of RPG arrived in Jakarta to conduct due diligence in May 1998. Jakarta was burning, and rioting and looting was going on everywhere. The director could not get into the city and was forced to return to England. At that time, Pramukti and Parwati were worried that he would not dare come back and complete the process.

Surprisingly, a week later, RPG returned to complete the due diligence and negotiation despite the warnings issued to travelers to avoid entering the country.

The IFC of the World Bank offered NISP a long-term loan and later converted the loan to NISP shares. NISP was the first bank in Indonesia to earn the trust of the IFC and to offer shares in an Indonesian bank to the IFC. The capital from the IFC and RPG strengthened both NISP's financial position and its spirit. This led to fantastic growth—an average of 30 percent per year despite the financial banking meltdown that plagued the country.

The trust that these international institutions had in NISP was a reflection of the confidence they had in the owner and employees of NISP.

Karmaka (left) with Mr. Lee Seng Wee,
OCBC major shareholder.

CHAPTER THIRTY-EIGHT

STRATEGIC DECISIONS

With an eleven-year-old transplanted liver, a single kidney, and cancerous tumors invading his urethra and urinary bladder, Karmaka, at age seventy-four, realized that his health would never be as it had been in the past. Nonetheless, he was very happy that he was still alive and well.

Moreover, Karmaka had miraculously safeguarded and nurtured NISP; under his guidance, the bank had grown from a savings bank in the city of Bandung to a commercial bank to a trusted partner of a leading foreign bank, Daiwa (now Resona of Japan), to a national commercial bank, and finally, NISP had become a foreign exchange bank. The journey continued, with NISP going public and being listed in the Indonesian Stock Exchange. NISP had reached its peak, as one of the ten biggest banks in Indonesia.

Karmaka remained the decision maker, while Pramukti and Parwati led the bank. Pramukti and Parwati were not satisfied with NISP being just a national commercial bank and insisted that NISP should continue to grow in the new Indonesian banking landscape. Pramukti had been suggesting to Karmaka that NISP strengthen its position against an increasing number of competitors, including those at the same level of the playing field in Southeast Asia.

After lengthy and serious discussions, Karmaka eventually agreed to bring in a new shareholder from overseas. At that time, the public already held 20 percent of NISP shares, and yet Pramukti and Parwati felt that NISP had to seek a shareholder who would be a strategic partner and hold a majority ownership. The strategic partner needed to be a strong regional or international bank.

With a strategic partner, NISP would be on more solid ground should there be another monetary crisis of any form. Also, without a strategic partner, in the climate of fierce global competition, NISP might not be able to fend off its competitors.

Pramukti made a strong argument for seeking a strategic partner, even though NISP was currently in a superior and stronger position. He noted that conducting the search when NISP was in an inferior and weak position would be unwise, as (1) the bank would have to conduct the search hastily, lowering its chances of selecting the right partner, and (2) with a weak bargaining position, its shares would be valued lower. For a long time, Karmaka had been holding onto aspirations for NISP to become one of the Big Five private banks of Indonesia. To this end, his children's desire for a strategic partnership seemed like the path to the realization of his dream.

Managing NISP's growth was another factor to be considered in the search for a strategic partner.. By that time, the bank had grown to two hundred branches with over three thousand employees and bank assets of more than 10 trillion rupiah. The need to upgrade NISP's management capability was obvious. At the moment, the management was too overburdened to carry out necessary tasks and the organization structure and systems were no longer suitable for the current stage of NISP's growth. In order to avoid the risks associated with developing on its own from the status quo, NISP, indeed, needed the systems and experience it could gain from a strategic partner.

Karmaka knew that Pramukti and Parwati's proposal was correct because their reasoning was rational and strong, but emotionally it was not easy for him to make the decision. Karmaka equated the loss of majority shares that would be a consequence of the strategic partnering with allowing NISP to be "swallowed" by a foreign bank. Given all the painstaking years during which Karmaka had sacrificed his body and soul—as well as his tears, sweat, and blood—his sentimental attachment to NISP was extremely strong.

It was only human for Karmaka to hesitate, to be fearful, and to be upset about having to make the decision. Such sentiment was common for the first generation of business founders. It was a sentiment full of mixed emotions and romanticism for which those who had poured their sweat and tears into building a business could not be blamed. To Karmaka, NISP was like his wife, children, breath, spirit, life, and death all rolled into one. How could he give up his very own being to an outsider?

"For three months I mulled over it, often with tears in my eyes," remembers Karmaka. "Yet, finally I had to be realistic and rational."

Even if they found a partner, the family would still own significant bank shares, despite no longer holding the majority. Furthermore, Karmaka and his children would still be very much involved in the management and decision making of the company.

Finally, Karmaka agreed to search for a strategic partner. Right away, his focus quickly shifted to formulating the partnership terms and conditions that would be favorable to the family and NISP's employees. A requirement that NISP's employees would not be laid off would be an absolute must. Karmaka did not want to once again feel the guilt associated with being responsible for a massive layoff of his loyal employees.

NISP conducted several meetings with prospective strategic partners from several international banks. The banks considered strategic partnerships with banks from Singapore, Hong Kong, the

Philippines, the United States, the Netherlands, France, and other countries. Karmaka felt lucky to have so many good choices, which indicated that NISP was able to attract a large variety of prospective partners. To Karmaka, strategic partnering was like a marriage—it was better to marry once and never file for divorce.

NISP had long known of the OCBC Group, Asia's leading financial service company based in Singapore. OCBC was well known for its prudence in management and for its very reputable majority shareholder partnerships with others. In addition, the group agreed to all of NISP's conditions, ensuring there would be no mass layoffs; therefore, Karmaka and the family decided to partner with OCBC. Accepting the no-layoff condition was precisely what OCBC wanted, as the group hoped to preserve NISP's culture of strong bonds between management and employees.

Karmaka had to admit that the people of OCBC had far-reaching views and acted in a gentlemanly manner during the negotiations. Even though OCBC held a 70 percent majority share, its management treated Karmaka and his family as equal partners. OCBC's management style did not include dictating to or ordering others around. Rather, OCBC managers listened to the opinions of the NISP employees.

At the onset of the partnership, Karmaka remained NISP's chairman, and his wife and eldest daughter remained members of the board of commissioners. Pramukti and Parwati stayed at their positions of CEO and deputy CEO. Four years later, OCBC Bank offered Karmaka a very honorable position—chairman emeritus; this was the first ever such position in Indonesia, and the bank made the offer in appreciation of Karmaka's past great merits and service as chairman. Furthermore, OCBC Bank asked the family to retain the positions of chairman and CEO of NISP. Pramukti took over his father's position as chairman, and Parwati filled the CEO vacancy. With this restructuring, Karmaka finally accomplished a smooth generational transition of leadership without any contention, a rare event indeed. OCBC Bank then requested that Karmaka continue to be active as senior advisor of the board of commissioners. With pride, Karmaka accepted his two new very respectable assignments.

The strategic partnership has been working very well, and Karmaka's family truly appreciated the trust OCBC management as the majority shareholders gave them. Karmaka and the family were committed to keep their trust.

Karmaka admitted that Pramukti and Parwati had indeed been wise in their thinking. He was very relieved and strongly believed that the future of NISP would be even better and brighter.

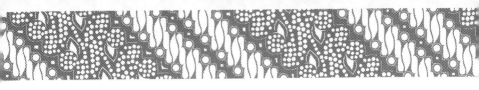

CHAPTER THIRTY-NINE

LOVE AND FAITH

With OCBC Bank as NISP's strategic partner, Karmaka could live a peaceful life in his old age, and he would be able to take regular care of his health without any stress from business pressures.

In 2006, his health deteriorated again. The continuous decline of the function of his remaining kidney threatened his health. Every day his feet felt cold, so cold that they cramped almost every night, which made sleeping difficult. His creatinine levels, a kidney function indicator, had reached a high of 7 mg/dL, a level that was dangerously higher than the normal level of 0.6 to 1.2 mg/dL. His hemoglobin level decreased to only 8 gm/dL, far below the normal level of 13 to 18 gm/dL. With blood infusions, his hemoglobin level rose for a while but subsequently dropped again. He needed continuous blood infusions to keep his hemoglobin count above a dangerous level.

However, with time, the infusions also lost their effectiveness. There was no other option. Karmaka needed a kidney transplant to replace his remaining left kidney. Since his right kidney had been removed a long time ago, there was no other remedy but to get a new kidney.

Thus, Karmaka was once again flown to the United States. Doctors informed him that to get a kidney transplant in the United States, he would have to wait several years, due to a short supply of kidney donors. With his rapidly deteriorating singly kidney, such a long waiting time would be dangerous for Karmaka. Karmaka conducted a search for a kidney in Japan and Hong Kong, where the doctors stated again and again that his illness was already too complicated and high risk, and thus, he would not outlive the wait.

Pramukti informed him that there was a thousand-year-old traditional healing practice in China called Zhen Qi that could be used to extend one's life. Pramukti wanted Karmaka to study the practice as a method for coping with the long waiting time. His efforts were successful. By practicing five hours a day, Karmaka was able to maintain his bodily function from day to day and month to month. To him, the discipline of the breathing practice was far from a boring routine. Rather, it was a means for his very survival.

After six long months during which Karmaka practiced Zhen Qi, a kidney donor was found. Karmaka was flown abroad again for the transplantation. Beyond all expectations, the transplant was very successful. It was a huge relief to all members of the family, because every doctor had told them that with Karmaka's worsening metabolic function and the condition of his body, he would not be able to survive the transplant.

After only three days, Karmaka was already able to walk and his urine was completely normal. The doctors and nurses congratulated him, surprised by their patient's rapid recovery. In three days, his kidney functions had already returned to normal, a process that normally takes ten days to two weeks.

Since Karmaka was now a double transplant patient, the doctor advised Karmaka to take the highest precautions, noting that he should not go directly home. He had to stay abroad for four months to prevent rejection or infection.

Unlike when he'd had his liver transplant (in the midst of the 1997 Asian monetary crisis), this time NISP was strong and stable, thanks to the strong strategic partnership with OCBC Bank. Therefore, Karmaka became "jobless" while abroad for an extended period of time.

However, he was not a person who could remain jobless. Karmaka spent his days keeping busy by writing. He wrote the whole story of his life, which would later become the material contained in this book.

When he returned to Indonesia, Karmaka was in perfect health. The employees of NISP, which by then numbered more than five thousand in 2007, welcomed Karmaka warmly. He was reminded of the similar welcome home party he'd enjoyed after his liver transplant ten years earlier.

By the end of 2008, the number of NISP branch offices had reached 370, and the bank's assets had reached 33 trillion rupiah (approximately US$3 billion). Karmaka's only wish was to be able to witness NISP become the fifth largest private bank in Indonesia, a desire he had had for long time.

Karmaka had endured multiple life-threatening illnesses in a span of thirty years. After enduring a burst gall bladder and liver transplant, he'd had his cancerous left kidney removed. By then, the cancer had spread to his urinary tract and bladder. He'd undergone catheter surgery to excise tumors in his bladder (as many as twenty-five within a three-year period). Finally, when his remaining right kidney had stopped functioning, he'd endured a kidney transplant. In addition, he had suffered a cracked thigh bone, followed by two surgeries to remove three cancerous lumps in his right ear. Miraculously, Karmaka survived the barrage of assaults on his body, eventually overcoming all of these illnesses.

Karmaka's endurance and longevity seemed miraculous. Many times, the gravity of his conditions had prompted doctors to pronounce that Karmaka's situation was "hopeless" based on their medical knowledge and experience. However, Karmaka was diligent and persistent in doing the exercises of Tai Qi Quan to keep his body and mind strong. The exercises and his strong will to live have endured, and Karmaka remains physically and mentally healthy as of the writing of this manuscript.

Karmaka's unrelenting illnesses never debilitated him. He was able to continue to work daily in his office for most of the time. Karmaka's character was strong in spirit and faith, attributes he'd probably gained because of his experiences as the eldest son in a poor family, sacrificing himself early in his life to overcome various challenges and support his family. Later in his life, he was rewarded by the support, attention, encouragement and tremendous love of his wife, children, son-in-law and grandchildren.

Karmaka's wife, Lelarati Lukman, was always by his side, managing the daily details of his life. She paid careful attention to Karmaka's daily consumption of food. She also made sure that Karmaka took his plethora of medications according to the appropriate schedules and dosages. Every night, she checked Karmaka's blood pressure. She transported him to checkups conducted in her clinical lab. She was always at Karmaka's side during his travels in search of treatments and during his many surgeries and therapies. Lelarati played a major role in Karmaka's ability to endure and survive his many trials. With the advice of her medical doctor daughter-in-law and son-in-law, Lelarati organized the search for medical consultations and doctors and helped Karmaka select the hospitals and surgeons who would treat him during the many years of battle with his illnesses. Karmaka always said that without Lelarati's love, care, and faith, he would not be alive today.

Lelarati is also a wife and mother extraordinaire. She always emphasized and prioritized the unity and harmony of the family. Without fail, Lelarati has been the central pillar of the family. Her beauty salon, which had been in continuous operation for forty-five years, a business she created and owns, carries her sentimental history. In its early years, the salon was the sole financial resource that supported the family, as well as the bank. She embodies the saying "Behind every great man is a great woman." Her entrepreneurship also resulted in a clinical laboratory business named Biotest, which has expanded into many cities of Indonesia and is managed by her with the help of her daughter, daughter-in-law, and son-in law.

Karmaka and his family are an example of how to deal successfully with life's struggles. They have shown the importance of planting self-worth, trust, and reputation and continuously cultivating these important attributes throughout life. Karmaka and his family are an example of how to implement a system of logical thinking, dare to accept challenges of any magnitude with courage, and never give up in the face of adversity with the hope of a better tomorrow. They exemplify the ability to work together to become a formidable force in overcoming any difficulties. Karmaka and his wife are a symbol of a sturdy marriage that can weather seemingly unending challenges.

In January 2009, Karmaka and Lelarati celebrated their golden wedding anniversary! Their children always say with pride that they are extraordinarily lucky to be born of parents who have dedicated themselves with unlimited love, care, and attention to their children's welfare and future. The couple has always placed their children as their highest priority, especially when it came to ensuring their education and preparation for the future. No matter how busy they were or how limited their financial resources were are at any time, the couple held firm to their commitment to take every measure to invest in their children's future. That way, their children would be rich in knowledge and upright in moral character, instead of being spoiled by unearned wealth that would eventually dry out without the skills of saving and earning more on their own for their lifetime and for future generations.

Family photo of the Surjaudajas, 1991.

Generational transition: (left to right)
Lerarati Lukman, Kamarka Surjaudaja, Parwati
Surjaudaja, & Pramukti Surjaudaja.

Children, In-laws, and grandchildren.

The next new generation-ten grandchildren.

WORDS OF THE CHILDREN

It is amazing how things happen. Our father, Karmaka Surjaudaja, who had had a liver transplant eleven years earlier, went to see *Pak* Dahlan, the author, to give him health tips related to his liver transplant. *Pak* Dahlan ended up writing our father's memoir. *Pak* Dahlan has said that he loves the book he wrote about our father because he wrote it from the heart. With such passion and sincerity, no wonder the book became an instant bestseller in Indonesia.

Pak Dahlan is a person of great integrity. He has proven himself to be a very successful entrepreneur and community leader. Our family is extremely grateful for his trust and is honored that he chose to write our father's life story. He is not only a very good friend but also an excellent example of a person who can build a huge and successful business based on hard work, honesty and open-mindedness. Given his remarkable accomplishments, it is not surprising that the Indonesian government asked him to become the CEO of PLN, the nation's electricity company. Dahlan did not need the job and only took on the responsibility out of love for his country, as he realizes that electricity is critical to the country's future. He does not use his position's facilities or benefits and has not taken a salary. Although the job has posed many difficult challenges, shortly after his arrival PLN underwent tremendous changes such as an overall significant increase in electricity up time for communities. Furthermore, during the recent top government revitalization, *Pak* Dahlan was appointed to have a much larger responsibility as the Minister of State-Owned Enterprises. We are extremely proud of him and have no doubt that he will do it with flying color. We also hope that he will take very good care of his health as that should be the most important thing for him, his family and the government.

No Such Thing as Can't received immediate attention from Indonesia's populace. The host of the most popular national TV talk show, *Kick Andy*, brought the book to a higher level of popularity when he interviewed both our father and *Pak* Dahlan on the writing of the book. Ever since then, many companies, organizations, and individuals have asked to meet with our father or offered him speaking engagements. We are also very proud to know, from the number of responses, that the book has inspired and motivated so many people in overcoming dire circumstances. Our father has personally signed over one thousand copies of the book.

Since the original publication of *No Such Thing as Can't* in Indonesian in 2009, Bank NISP has made further strategic changes. Firstly, its name has been changed from Bank NISP to Bank OCBC NISP as the result of a strong, trusting partnership with OCBC Bank of Singapore; highly compatible business cultures connect the two banks. Secondly, to strengthen the impact, Bank OCBC NISP merged with the existing parent bank's subsidiary in Indonesia, Bank OCBC Indonesia. The surviving bank carries the name of Bank OCBC NISP. No doubt the new entity will be much strengthened with full support and further development by the parent Bank OCBC of Singapore. To date, the bank has over four hundred offices with six hundred self-owned ATM outlets. All stakeholders, including customers, employees, and shareholders benefit significantly from these changes.

The family continues to manage the newly established entity, with Parwati as its CEO and Pramukti as its chairman. Karmaka remains chairman emeritus and senior advisor to the board. In March 2011, our seventy-year-old mother voluntarily resigned as a board member and was elected Senior Advisor and Commissioner Emeritus, the first time in Indonesian banking industry that such a title has been conferred, in recognition of her significant role during the last thirty years.

The medical diagnostic laboratory, Biotest, an enterprise founded by our mother, has been strengthened since its inception thirty years ago. Now it has eight fully integrated medical diagnostic laboratories equipped with the most modern equipment and strategically located in major cities of Indonesia with a commitment to providing excellent services. Over twelve thousand medical doctors in Indonesia and fifty medical doctors in Singapore have chosen Biotest. Biotest also has over a thousand corporate clients, ranging from national to international companies, including major state-owned enterprises.

Dr. Simon Rusmin, our father's best childhood friend, translated this book from its Indonesian version into English, and Dr. Rusmin's two daughters, Ruru Rusmin and Delia Rusmin, who reside in the United States, reviewed it. Dr. Simon graduated from Bandung Institute of Technology in Indonesia and obtained his PhD in life sciences from the University of Kentucky. He has had a long career in quality assurance in the pharmaceutical industry in the United States and has consulted with many major companies in different countries.

It is our hope that that the English version of the book, published in 2011, will also inspire many more people to believe that there is *No Such Thing as Can't*!